"The church in the West is experiencing a lull in evangelism at a time when the need has never been greater—nor the opportunity brighter—for the church to tell the world the good news in Jesus. In *God Shines Forth*, Daniel Hames and Michael Reeves take us to the heart of the biblical motivation to share Christ: a proper vision of our great and glorious God. The more we are overflowing with the glorious love of God, the more we will overflow with words of the gospel to others. This book will show you how to overflow with gospel love."

Ed Stetzer, Executive Director, Wheaton College Billy Graham Center

"I could hardly put this book down—it made my heart sing. *God Shines Forth* is an immensely joyful and faith-building encouragement to all who love and long to enjoy and participate in God's mission."

Gloria Furman, coeditor, *Joyfully Spreading the Word*; author, *Missional Motherhood*

"After decades of mission work, I've witnessed the various motivations driving missionary efforts, from the worst (a guilty conscience or vain ambition) to the good (a genuine concern for the lost). But Hames and Reeves call us to remember the best: that knowing and loving God deeply, fully, with a reckless abandon is our first and most essential priority for missions. They make it clear that when we truly know the nature of our loving, giving, gracious God, when we delight in him, we have the true fuel from God for missions. Don't let anyone you know go to the mission field without reading this book."

J. Mack Stiles, former Pastor, Erbil Baptist Church, Iraq

"The big idea of this book is both simple and life-transforming: 'It is precisely *because* God is outgoing and communicative that he is so good and delightful.' Thus, as this God's beloved people delight in him, they are propelled to speak about his goodness to others by communicating the good news. Yes, evangelism is a biblically commanded duty for all Christians. Yes, the Great Commission is a scripturally grounded purpose of the church. Yes, missions is a theologically supported enterprise for the benefit of the world. Ultimately, however, this endeavor is an overflow from knowing God. This book gets this truth right!"

Gregg R. Allison, Professor of Christian Theology, The Southern Baptist Theological Seminary; Secretary, Evangelical Theological Society; author, *Historical Theology*; *Sojourners and Strangers*; and *Embodied*

"Missiology tends to be long on pragmatics and short on theology. What a mistake! This book grounds our missiology in our theology, and provides a vision for how the truths of the Bible shape us and authentically motivate us toward the Great Commission."

Josh Moody, Senior Pastor, College Church, Wheaton, Illinois; President and Founder, God Centered Life Ministries

GOD SHINES FORTH

Union

A book series edited by Michael Reeves

Rejoice and Tremble: The Surprising Good News of the Fear of the Lord, Michael Reeves (2021)

What Does It Mean to Fear the Lord?, Michael Reeves (2021, concise version of *Rejoice and Tremble*)

Deeper: Real Change for Real Sinners, Dane C. Ortlund (2021)

How Does God Change Us?, Dane C. Ortlund (2021, concise version of *Deeper*)

The Loveliest Place: The Beauty and Glory of the Church, Dustin Benge (2022)

Why Should We Love the Local Church?, Dustin Benge (2022, concise version of *The Loveliest Place*)

God Shines Forth: How the Nature of God Shapes and Drives the Mission of the Church, Daniel Hames and Michael Reeves (2022)

What Fuels the Mission of the Church?, Daniel Hames and Michael Reeves (2022, concise version of *God Shines Forth*)

6/5/24

Daren & Janelle,
So thankful for how God is
using you to impact lives in
needy places. May His glory
continue to shine brightly
through you.

Pastor
Glen

GOD
SHINES
FORTH

*How the Nature of God Shapes and
Drives the Mission of the Church*

DANIEL HAMES AND
MICHAEL REEVES

:: CROSSWAY®

WHEATON, ILLINOIS

God Shines Forth: How the Nature of God Shapes and Drives the Mission of the Church
Copyright © 2022 by Daniel Hames and Michael Reeves
Published by Crossway
      1300 Crescent Street
      Wheaton, Illinois 60187

Cover design: Jordan Singer

Cover image: Photo © Christie's Images / Bridgeman Images

First printing 2022

Printed in the United States of America

Hardcover ISBN: 978-1-4335-7514-3
ePub ISBN: 978-1-4335-7517-4
PDF ISBN: 978-1-4335-7515-0
Mobipocket ISBN: 978-1-4335-7516-7

Library of Congress Cataloging-in-Publication Data

Names: Hames, Daniel, author. | Reeves, Michael (Michael Richard Ewert), author.
Title: God shines forth : how the nature of God shapes and drives the mission of the church / Daniel Hames and Michael Reeves.
Description: Wheaton, Illinois : Crossway, 2022. | Series: Union | Includes bibliographical references and index.
Identifiers: LCCN 2022005075 (print) | LCCN 2022005076 (ebook) | ISBN 9781433575143 (hardcover) | ISBN 9781433575150 (pdf) | ISBN 9781433575167 (mobipocket) | ISBN 9781433575174 (epub)
Subjects: LCSH: Spirituality—Christianity. | Mission of the church. | Missions—Theory.
Classification: LCC BV4501.3 .H3535 2022 (print) | LCC BV4501.3 (ebook) | DDC 266—dc23/eng/20220414
LC record available at https://lccn.loc.gov/2022005075
LC ebook record available at https://lccn.loc.gov/2022005076

Crossway is a publishing ministry of Good News Publishers.

VP   31   30   29   28   27   26   25   24   23   22
15   14   13   12   11   10   9   8   7   6   5   4   3   2   1

For Paul and Janey Hames
Psalm 113

The Mighty One, God the LORD,
    speaks and summons the earth
    from the rising of the sun to its setting.
Out of Zion, the perfection of beauty,
    God shines forth.

PSALM 50:1–2

Contents

Series Preface

OUR INNER CONVICTIONS AND VALUES shape our lives and our ministries. And at Union—the cooperative ministries of Union School of Theology, Union Publishing, Union Research, and Union Mission (visit www.theolo.gy)—we long to grow and support men and women who will delight in God, grow in Christ, serve the church, and bless the world. This Union series of books is an attempt to express and share those values.

They are values that flow from the beauty and grace of God. The living God is so glorious and kind, he cannot be known without being adored. Those who truly know him will love him, and without that heartfelt delight in God, we are nothing but hollow hypocrites. That adoration of God necessarily works itself out in a desire to grow in Christlikeness. It also fuels a love for Christ's precious bride, the church, and a desire humbly to serve—rather than use—her. And, lastly, loving God brings us to share his concerns, especially to see his life-giving glory fill the earth.

Each exploration of a subject in the Union series will appear in two versions: a full volume and a concise one. The idea is that church leaders can read the full treatment, such as this one, and so delve into each topic while making the more accessible concise version widely available to their congregations.

My hope and prayer is that these books will bless you and your church as you develop a deeper delight in God that overflows in joyful integrity, humility, Christlikeness, love for the church, and a passion to make disciples of all nations.

Michael Reeves
SERIES EDITOR

Introduction

The Great Admission

LET'S GET IT OUT IN THE OPEN right at the beginning. Doesn't something about mission and evangelism just feel "off" to you? Every Christian knows we're meant to share the gospel and look for opportunities to witness to Christ, yet almost all of us find it a genuine struggle, if not a gloomy discouragement. The vital, final thing Jesus left his followers to do—the Great Commission!—seems to be the one thing about the Christian life that, frankly, doesn't feel so great. While we've heard the motivational sermons, sat in the "how to" seminars, and tried to crank ourselves up to initiating a deep conversation with friends or colleagues, the whole enterprise tends to flood us with dread rather than enthusiasm. And that leaves us feeling awkward and ashamed.

Complicating matters is that most of us *do* have a sincere desire that the people we love would come to know the Lord as we do. When we give even a moment's thought to the blessings of the Christian life now, let alone the hope of eternity with Christ, we hope and pray with real feeling that our loved ones might come to saving faith. The thing is that this longing doesn't seem to translate very easily or very often into actual evangelism. Any passion and boldness we may have in prayer apparently evaporates under the spotlight at the dinner table or on the coffee break. Our words dry up, our confidence deserts us, and we could wish we were almost anywhere else in the world.

If this all sounds familiar to you, you are not alone. Christians the world over will recognize your guilty gulp when evangelism is mentioned in the pulpit. We all experience the strange tension you've felt between the *theory* of cheerfully sharing the good news and the *reality* of frantically retreating and locking the door behind you. So, what is going on? What is the mysterious cause of our complicated relationship with mission?

Mission Fatigue

Some Christians have decided to dispense with evangelism altogether, because they believe it to be downright inappropriate. The Barna Group found in 2019 that 47 percent of Christian millennials (defined here as those between ages twenty and thirty-four) believe "it is wrong to share one's personal beliefs with someone of a different faith in hopes that they will one day share the same faith."[1] After all, is it really any of our business who goes to hell?[2] Surely, they argue, it's the epitome of pride to press oneself and one's God onto another person. Within mainline denominations, "born again Christians" who believe in such "conversion" are sometimes looked on with suspicion as oddball fundamentalists. In 1993 representatives of the Roman Catholic and Orthodox Churches drafted the Balamand

---

1 "Almost Half of Practicing Christian Millennials Say Evangelism Is Wrong," Barna (website), February 5, 2019, https://www.barna.com.

2 Brian D. McLaren, *A New Kind of Christian: A Tale of Two Friends on a Spiritual Journey* (Hoboken, NJ: John Wiley, 2001), chap. 14.

Document, which included an agreement not to seek "conversion of persons from one Church to the other," calling it a "source of proselytism."[3] This was a moratorium on mission.

Meanwhile, some argue that certain groups are out of bounds when it comes to mission. In 2002, the United States Conference of Catholic Bishops produced a report on Catholic-Jewish relations, which concluded that "campaigns that target Jews for conversion to Christianity are no longer theologically acceptable in the Catholic Church."[4] Similarly, in 2015, the Vatican's Commission for Religious Relations with Jews published a document that made it clear "the Catholic Church neither conducts nor supports any specific institutional mission work directed towards Jews."[5] In the secular world, attempting to bring someone else over to faith in Christ may once have been viewed as impolite or crass: now it may be regarded as something far more sinister. With the history of Western missionaries importing European culture to Africa and Asia, forced conversions, the complicity of the German church in the Holocaust, and Christians' generally conservative social outlook, the spread of Christianity is seen as a means of oppression. Christian mission is associated by some with imperialism, White supremacy, and the hegemony of the powerful over minority groups. Brian D. McLaren argues that evangelism has historically been "a proclamation of the superiority of the Christian religion."[6]

3   "Uniatism, Method of Union of the Past, and the Present Search for Full Communion," Pontifical Council for Promoting Christian Unity, June 23, 1993, http://www.christianunity.va/, 10, 15.
4   Consultation of the National Council of Synagogues and Delegates of the Bishops Committee for Ecumenical and Interreligious Affairs, "Reflections on Covenant and Mission" (PDF), August 12, 2002, 1.
5   Commission for Religious Relations with Jews, "The Gifts and Calling of God Are Irrevocable," EWTN (website), December, 10, 2015, https://www.ewtn.com/catholicism, 6.40.
6   Brian D. McLaren, *A New Kind of Christianity: Ten Questions That Are Transforming the Faith* (London: HarperOne, 2010), 216.

These intellectual and cultural sensitivities might be on the radar for some of us, but they are almost certainly not the real root of our internal nagging discomfort about mission. They may be a hindrance, but they don't get to the bottom of what we're feeling. It's possible that other explanations come closer to the mark. Perhaps insecurity keeps us from evangelism. We worry what other people might think of us if we start "Bible-thumping," so we keep quiet. Or perhaps our problem is fear of failure. We don't feel well enough equipped or aren't confident enough in the power of the gospel, so we dare not risk rejection or (perhaps worse) indifference. Again, these things may play a part in our predicament, but the diagnosis still doesn't quite fit the symptoms. Cultural pressure, personal insecurity, or fear of failure seems to presuppose a burning passion in us to share the gospel that is simply being inhibited by some external barriers needing to be removed. A little training or a good pep talk could have us out on the streets in no time, fulfilling our hearts' desire to proclaim Christ every moment of every day!

But here is the great admission that many of us need to make: when it comes to the Great Commission, our *hearts* aren't really in it. Something far deeper than practical or operational limitations is causing our mission fatigue. What ails us goes right to the core of our relationship with God.

Here's the Catch

If we are entirely honest, when we think about evangelism, we often feel something close to resentment. Many of us silently grumble that, in being recruited to evangelism, we're being put upon. We first came to know Jesus very happily, receiving his mercy and his invitation to new life, but then along came this unexpected and slightly puzzling additional step of having to be a witness to him in the world. Like a car shifting into the wrong gear, we came to a juddering halt. We'd been *offered* free grace and forgiveness, but now there's a *demand?* Christianity, we fear, was just too good to be true. Mission is the inevitable catch tacked on to the list of benefits we signed up for. It's the complicated and rather unwelcome add-on to salvation that God has included in the deal as the sweetener for himself.

So we imagine that, in our salvation, God has done his part, and with that dealt with, he now sits in his heaven with his feet up while we are left below with what seems like the hard, dirty work of mission. Psalm 96:3 says,

Declare his glory among the nations,
    his marvelous works among all the peoples!

Isaiah 12:4 is similar:

Give thanks to the LORD,
    call upon his name,
make known his deeds among the peoples,
    proclaim that his name is exalted.

There is simply no avoiding these clear commands of Scripture. God wants us to make him known in the world. This is our responsibility and our work as Christians. Jesus only adds to the task when he says that, as well as making him known, we're to persuade other people to become his obedient followers: "All authority in heaven and on earth has been given to me. Go therefore and make disciples of all nations, baptizing them in the name of the Father and of the Son and of the Holy Spirit, *teaching them to observe all that I have commanded you*" (Matt. 28:18–20). As if the pressure weren't enough already, Paul writes that the fate of the world is dependent on our broadcasting the message, for "how are they to hear without someone preaching?" (Rom. 10:14).

So it seems that the Christian is left with no choice. In light of everything God has done for us, we owe him—and this is what he's stipulated. So we buckle in, brace ourselves, and make the occasional attempt at sharing the gospel, when we can bear it. Like stepping into a cold shower, we grit our teeth and get it over with.

When encouragements come from our snatched evangelistic conversations or a friend agrees to come to church with us, we reveal our true approach by our secret reactions. We tell ourselves we've ticked the evangelism box or met our mission quota, paying off little installments on our debt to the Lord. Now we have something holy sounding to report to our church friends. We pat ourselves on the back for our moment of pious bravery.

Nevertheless, having been drawn in by promises of easy yokes and light burdens, we have the sensation of being trapped in a contractual obligation. The thought of enjoying God forever had sounded warm and inviting, but the very word *evangelism* can send a chill down the spine. It makes the whole dynamic of the Christian life—even the very gospel we tout as such good news—seem almost distasteful. The worst of it is that all this ultimately reflects very badly on God, who begins not to look so good and attractive as we first thought. Like a PR agency representing a difficult client, we begin to wonder what we've got ourselves into. This reveals the real issue. The problem at the root of all our struggles with mission is almost certainly right at the beginning: with our view of God.

Getting God Right

If we believe that God is simply out to impose himself on the world and suck it dry of glory and praise, then we will never love and want to share him (even if we tell ourselves that God is entitled to do whatever he wants). If God seems to us a demanding taskmaster, we will never be his eager ambassadors in the world. If we feel ourselves conned into having to perform evangelism, we will never warm to the calling he has set before us. Unless we honestly find God to be beautiful and enjoyable, we'll have nothing worth saying to the people around us. Until we see him aright, we'll have no genuine desire to fill the world with the knowledge of our God.

This book, then, is not a practical "how to" guide for mission, devoted to the methodology of evangelism and how Christians can best equip themselves for it. Nor is it a biblical theology of mission, exploring the scriptural contours of calling, sending, and the growth of the kingdom of God. Plenty of good books do these things already. This book is an invitation to start again at the beginning with your vision of God. Our aim is to set before your eyes God as he truly is: God who is so full of life and goodness that he loves to be known; not as a campaign to *impose* himself on us or on the world but to *give* himself and *share* his own life with the world. We want to show that the God of mission is no different from the God of the gospel. In fact, it is precisely *because* God is outgoing and communicative that he is so good and delightful. His natural fullness and superabundance mean that he does not need to *take* or *demand* from us but freely and kindly loves to *bless* us. His mission is not to wring out the world for every last drop but to *fill* it with his own divine joy and beauty. Seeing *this* glorious God will change everything for us.

Mission is no clunky add-on to your own delighting in God. Instead, it is the natural overflow and expression of the enjoyment you have of him so that, *like him*, you gladly go out to fill the world with the word of his goodness. None of us can drum up enthusiasm for "mission" as an abstract activity to be gotten on with, especially if it's caked in all kinds of negative assumptions and worries. But to see God as he really is is to delight in him. And as we grow in the knowledge and love of this God, we'll find blossoming in ourselves his own desire to see the world filled with his blessing.

William Tyndale once described the gospel as "good, merry, glad and joyful tidings, that maketh a man's heart glad, and maketh him sing, dance and leap for joy . . . [for] which tidings, as many as believe, laud, praise and thank God."[7] The surge of happiness we know, as we appreciate God in his radiant kindness, is one and the same movement that opens our mouths in praise and proclamation. Our going out to the world with the gospel is not an endeavor that Christians have to hitch on to knowing God, bringing to the task a vigor and vim outsourced from elsewhere. Rather, the heart-gladdening, feet-quickening reality of God is itself at once all the motivation, the content, and the zest of our going. It is precisely because God, from his own glorious fullness, fills us with joy in him that we begin to bubble over with it to those around. This is the *theological* dynamic of mission. The wellspring of healthy, happy mission is God himself.

---

7   William Tyndale, *A Pathway into the Holy Scripture*, in *The Works of the English Reformers: William Tyndale and John Frith*, ed. Thomas Russell, vol. 2 (London: Palmer, 1831), 490.

1

The Glory of God

HAPPY MISSION PRESUPPOSES HAPPY CHRISTIANS.

There is a kind of mission that can be carried out by miserable Christians, and though it may be doctrinally correct and carefully organized, it will only reflect the emptiness in their own hearts. Christians who don't *enjoy* God can't and won't wholeheartedly commend him to others. If we fear that God's love for us is reluctant or that his approval rests on our performance, we won't feel any real affection for him, our service will be grudging, and the world will likely see through us.

This was the experience of Martin Luther as a young monk who, though profoundly devoted and spiritually zealous, was nevertheless filled with dread at the thought of God. "I did not love, yes, I hated the righteous God," he confessed, "and secretly, if not blasphemously, certainly murmuring greatly, I was angry with God."[1] Two hundred years later, Jonathan Edwards, also an intensely religious young man, was racked with "concerns and exercises about [his] soul" and recoiled

---

†   Martin Luther, "Preface to the Complete Edition of Luther's Latin Writings," in *Luther's Works*, vol. 34, *Career of the Reformer IV*, ed. Lewis William Spitz and Helmut T. Lehmann (Philadelphia: Fortress; St. Louis, MO: Concordia, 1960), 336–37.

from the "horrible doctrine" of God's sovereignty.[2] These were deeply unhappy men trying to be Christians.

Luther and Edwards both underwent transformations in their views of God that lit up their lives, melted their hard hearts, and fueled years of sincerely *joyful* ministry. Both discovered—and then preached, taught, and wrote about—a God who is delightfully good. Carrying them through illness, loss, persecution, and poverty, their fresh understanding of God truly changed everything for them. At the heart of their happy Christianity was the realization that knowing God rightly must always begin with Jesus Christ.

Step into the Light

A whole array of spiritual paths and philosophical traditions claims to give us clarity on what God is and is not like, but Jesus declares himself the unique and totally sufficient gateway to God. "I am the way, and the truth, and the life," he says. "No one comes to the Father except through me" (John 14:6). In fact, the knowledge of God is *hidden* from "the wise and understanding" and must be "*revealed*" (Matt. 11:25–26). Even those we might expect to have the most intelligent, imaginative thoughts about God cannot know about him unless he shows himself. Jesus says, "All things have been handed over to me by my Father, and no one knows the Son except the Father, and no one knows the Father except the Son and anyone to whom the Son chooses to reveal him" (Matt. 11:27).

The truth of God is naturally hidden from the world in the closed loop of relationship between the Father and the Son, and none of us can guess our way in. Only the Son, the one who knows the Father,

---

2 Jonathan Edwards, *The Works of Jonathan Edwards*, vol. 16, *Letters and Personal Writings*, ed. George S. Claghorn (New Haven, CT: Yale University Press, 1998), 790.

can open this knowledge to us. In Jesus Christ alone, "in whom are hidden all the treasures of wisdom and knowledge" (Col. 2:3), do we see God as he truly is. Jesus puts this rather specific (even exclusive) approach down to his Father's "gracious will" (Matt. 11:26) and clearly does not see it as a means to privilege an elite few over the masses, for his very next words are as inclusive an invitation as we could imagine: "Come to me, all who labor and are heavy laden, and I will give you rest" (Matt. 11:28). Anyone can come to know the living God and find rest in him, but it is uniquely to *Jesus* they must come.

All this is encapsulated when Paul calls Jesus "the image of the invisible God" (Col. 1:15). He is the one who stepped into the world he had created, showing us the God we could not see by ourselves. John also carries this theme with his title for the Son, "the Word" who was "in the beginning" with his Father (John 1:1). Just as our words reveal and expose who and what we are (Luke 6:45), God's Word—his eternal Son—perfectly expresses and reveals him. This Word is also "the true *light*, which gives light to everyone" (John 1:9). Here we meet a very common scriptural theme: that of the Son *enlightening* us. John here is clearly drawing on the light "in the beginning" of Genesis 1:3. Paul does the same in 2 Corinthians 4 when he speaks of "the *light* of the gospel of the glory of Christ, who is the image of God" (v. 4). Indeed, he writes that "God, who said, 'Let light shine out of darkness,' has *shone in our hearts* to give the light of the knowledge of the glory of God *in the face of Jesus Christ*" (v. 6).

Time and again, Scripture is clear that sinful humanity languishes in unknowing darkness, and, left to our imaginations, we dream up a miserable god, quite deserving of our dislike and mistrust. The unique and cheering work of Jesus is to be the light in the dark rooms of our hearts and minds, showing us the Father. As John Calvin put it, "We are blind as to the light of God, until in Christ it beams on us."[3]

Source and Beam

To get a right and true understanding of God (and to correct any faults and distortions we may continue to pick up) we must look to the Son. But when Jesus reveals his Father to us, he is not just passing on information about God. Because Jesus *is* himself God—the eternal Son of the Father—he is God *with* us. Not an expert lecturer or detailed commentator we may learn from, but God in person, reaching out to us to be known by us.

The writer to the Hebrews describes Jesus as the "exact imprint" or perfect representation of God to us, and also "the radiance of the glory of God" (1:3). To speak of Jesus as the "radiance" of God's glory is to say that Jesus is not a light directed at some *other* subject, like a flashlight pointed at your shoes in a tent at night. Radiance, like the sun and its beams, speaks of something—or someone—that, by nature, shines out and *gives* light. In other words, it is not that God is hiding in the dark and we must enlist Jesus to help us seek him out. Rather, God himself *is* the source of that light that comes to us in Christ. Put another way, the light that shines on us in Jesus *is* the light of the Father. The Father and the Son are one being, one God. The eternal life of God *is* the Father begetting his Son in the Holy Spirit. What we see in Jesus is not peripheral to the being of God. No, the Father, radiating his Son, shines like the sun in the sky and, by those beams, communicates himself to us. "God is light," writes John, "and in him is no darkness at all" (1 John 1:5), and so

3 John Calvin, *Calvin's Commentaries*, vol. 22, *Calvin's Commentaries on the Epistle of Paul the Apostle to the Hebrews*, trans. John Owen (Grand Rapids, MI: Baker, 1989), on Heb. 1:3.

his Son is "the light of the world" (John 8:12). The Puritan preacher Thomas Goodwin saw this and said, "The sun doth not only enrich the earth with all good things . . . but glads and refreshes all with shedding immediately its own wings of light and warmth, which is so pleasant to behold and enjoy. And thus doth God, and Christ the Sun of righteousness."[4]

In the radiance of Jesus, we not only are learning something *about* God but are *receiving God himself.* To see God rightly, to whom else would we turn?

Jesus, the Glory of God

This brings us to the language of "glory" that we have only danced around so far as we considered the light of God's self-revelation in Jesus. It is there in John 1 as John writes, "We have seen his *glory,* glory as of the only Son from the Father" (v. 14); it is there in 2 Corinthians 4, where Christians are given "the light of the knowledge of the *glory of God* in the face of Jesus Christ" (v. 6). B. B. Warfield wrote that more than a simple association is being made between Jesus and glory. Yes, Jesus came *from* glory (John 17:5), returned *to* his glory (1 Tim. 3:16), and will come *again* in glory (Titus 2:13), but "we come nearer to what is implied when we read of Jesus being 'the Lord *of* glory' (1 Cor 2:8), that is He to whom glory belongs as His characterizing quality; or when He is described to us as 'the effulgence of the glory of God' (Heb 1:3)."[5] Jesus is not only glorious in a *descriptive* way; he is God's Glory in a *definitive* way. As we have

---

4 Thomas Goodwin, *The Works of Thomas Goodwin*, vol. 1, *An Exposition of the First Chapter of the Epistle to the Ephesians* (Edinburgh: Nichol, 1861), 46.

5 Benjamin. B. Warfield, *The Lord of Glory: A Study of the Designations of Our Lord in the New Testament with Especial Reference to His Deity* (New York: American Tract Society, 1907), 264 (emphasis added).

seen, for the writer to the Hebrews, Jesus *is* the Glory of God: the very outshining radiance of his being.

The Greek word for "glory" here, δόξα (*doxa*), was classically used to mean an accepted belief or opinion about someone or that person's reputation. It comes from the verb "appear" or "seem." In the New Testament, though, the word was filled with a slightly different sense. It picked up all the resonances of the Old Testament Hebrew word for glory, כָּבוֹד (*kavod*). This word literally means "weight" or "copiousness"—the sheer, unmissable presence of something, especially in bright, shining splendor. So the shepherds outside Bethlehem watched over their flocks by night when "the glory of the Lord *shone* around them" (Luke 2:9). And the new Jerusalem, we read, does not need the sun or the moon to shine on it, "for the glory of God *gives it light*" (Rev. 21:23). Edwards speaks of glory as "an effulgence, or shining brightness, by an emanation of beams of light."[6] Glory is the weight and reality of a thing *shining* out, or being brought home to us, reaching us irresistibly. For Jesus Christ to be the "radiance of the glory of God" is for him to be the weight or the substance of God impressed upon us, beaming on us, *given* to us.

John's wonder is palpable at the start of his first letter as he writes about seeing with his own eyes and touching with his hands the one who was "from the beginning" and "with the Father" but is now "made manifest to us" (1 John 1:1–2). The one whom John and his fellow disciples have walked and talked with, held in their arms, and known as a friend is the one who was eternally at the Father's side but now is seen, made known, and given. When John went with Peter

---

6 Jonathan Edwards, "The End for Which God Created the World," in *The Works of Jonathan Edwards*, vol. 8, *Ethical Writings*, ed. Paul Ramsey (New Haven, CT: Yale University Press, 1989), 516.

and James up the mountain and saw the Lord transfigured, they saw his face shine like the sun, and even his clothes became "white as light" (Matt. 17:2). While they marveled as he spoke with Moses and Elijah, "a bright cloud overshadowed them, and a voice from the cloud said, 'This is my beloved Son, with whom I am well pleased; listen to him'" (Matt. 17:5).

Amid all the brightness and light, what is trumpeted most clearly is the Father's complete approval of his Son. Nothing and nobody else could more completely unveil, display, and thus please God the Father. That the Son is his Father's Glory will be shown when eventually all creation will recognize Jesus as Lord, "to the *glory* of God the Father" (Phil. 2:11). In Jesus, we see the very being of God shining forth on us.

The Glory of Israel

Jesus's transfiguration picks up a significant Old Testament thread. When the Lord appeared to his people, he frequently appeared in the כָּבוֹד (*kavod*) of shining light or blazing fire along with billowing cloud and the sound of thunder. His presence with his people is an apocalyptic, electrical storm of grandeur.

> Now the appearance of the glory of the LORD was like a devouring fire on the top of the mountain in the sight of the people of Israel. (Ex. 24:17)

> Arise, shine, for your light has come,
>   and the glory of the LORD has risen upon you.
> For behold, darkness shall cover the earth,
>   and thick darkness the peoples;
> but the LORD will arise upon you,
>   and his glory will be seen upon you. (Isa. 60:1–2)

The house was filled with the cloud, and the court was filled with the brightness of the glory of the LORD. (Ezek. 10:4)

In rabbinic writing, this shining glory was sometimes called the *shekinah*. The word isn't found in Scripture, but it comes from the Hebrew שָׁכֵן (*shakan*), "dwell" or "settle," which we do find in the Old Testament. In Deuteronomy 33:16, Moses blesses the family of Joseph with "the favor of him who *dwells* in the bush"—poignantly recalling the day the angel of the Lord appeared to him "in a flame of fire out of the midst of a bush" (Ex. 3:2). Jonathan Edwards says that, when we read of the glory of God shining visibly in instances like this, we are to understand more than just a mysterious golden sheen being cast over everything. Rather, the brightness and light that Moses and others saw emanated from a *person* who appeared to them.[7] The Lord himself, who is called "the Glory of Israel" in 1 Samuel 15:29, was coming to be near to Moses, to be seen, and to converse with them. Ezekiel spoke of seeing the glory of the Lord "standing" before him, as a person would (3:23). For this reason, Edwards argues that the Old Testament phrase "the Glory of the Lord" is frequently a title of God the Son in his appearances to the prophets and patriarchs—"a distinct person from the first in the Godhead" who comes to dwell among the Israelites.[8]

In Isaiah 3:8, the people are said to have provoked the eyes of God's glory, plainly speaking of the glory of the Lord as a *person*. In the book of Ezekiel, [we] read of the glory of the Lord ascending from and descending into the temple (Ezekiel 8:4,

---

7   Jonathan Edwards, *The Works of Jonathan Edwards*, vol. 21, *Writings on the Trinity, Grace, and Faith*, ed. Sang Hyun Lee (New Haven, CT: Yale University Press, 2003), 374.
8   Edwards, *Works*, 21:374.

and Ezekiel 9:3, and Ezekiel 10:18–19, and Ezekiel 11:22, and Ezekiel 43:2). God the Father dwelt in heaven, but his glory dwelt on earth.[9]

The one who appeared to Moses in the burning bush then led Israel through the Red Sea and the wilderness, traveling in the fiery, cloudy pillar that "lit up the night" around them (Ex. 14:19–21). He scattered their enemies and rescued them (Ex. 14:24). Later, it was the Lord in the cloud who moved into the Most Holy Place in the finished tabernacle, filling it with his glory (Ex. 40:34–35). There in the tabernacle, the Lord dwelt permanently among the people of Israel, enthroned on the ark of the covenant and its cherubim-ornamented lid. Whether in that tent or in the later temple in Jerusalem, the Lord promised he would "appear in the cloud over the mercy seat" (Lev. 16:2), there to receive the sacrifices and worship of the people, so that the psalmist could cry out to him, "You who are enthroned upon the cherubim, shine forth" (Ps. 80:1).

The glory of God is *personal*: the Father's radiance is the Son. It is God the Son who comes to be with his people and, in doing so, shines upon us the truth of the Father.

In a similar vein, Edwards takes "the Name of the Lord" to be a title of the Son, speaking of his revelation of God's nature to his people.[10] Since Isaiah says "the name of the LORD comes from afar, / burning with his anger" (30:27), the name of the Lord is conceived of as a person who can be angry, who can travel and speak.[11] God's name is "in him" (Ex. 23:21), and the temple is to

---

9 Edwards, *Works*, 21:379 (emphasis added).
10 Edwards, *Works*, 21:372.
11 Edwards, *Works*, 21:377.

be "a house for [his] name" (2 Sam. 7:13). In Psalm 20:1–2 it is the "name of the God of Jacob" who is to protect his people, sending "help from the sanctuary" in Zion.[12]

This seems to be the understanding of the early Christians in the book of Acts, who rejoice to be "counted worthy to suffer dishonor for *the name*" (5:41). In these titles for the Son, we are learning about God's intention to be present intimately with sinful, wayward people through the Son, who mediates, reveals, and dwells among us. Though we live in ignorance and darkness, in the Son, the Father speaks, saves, and shines out.

Face-to-Face

Perhaps the most striking passage to illustrate this is Exodus 33, where Moses, fresh from receiving the law on Sinai, has returned to find the Israelites worshiping an idol. In frustration and fear, Moses asks God for a sign that he is still in his favor and that he will not be left alone to shepherd so hopeless a crowd. Moses pleads to know God's ways (v. 13) and to see God's glory (v. 18). The Lord replies, "You cannot see my face, for man shall not see me and live" (v. 20); "my face shall not be seen" (v. 23). But God agrees to pass before Moses, with the proviso that Moses will need to be hidden in a rock and covered if he is not to die (vv. 21–22).

On first reading, this seems odd because, just verses earlier, we read:

> When Moses entered the tent, the pillar of cloud would descend and stand at the entrance of the tent, and the LORD would speak with Moses. And when all the people saw the pillar of cloud standing at the entrance of the tent, all the people would rise up and

12 Edwards, *Works*, 21:376–77.

worship, each at his tent door. *Thus the LORD used to speak to Moses face to face, as a man speaks to his friend* (vv. 9–11).

How can these two passages sit in the same chapter of the Bible? Edwards writes that, once again, there is here the mediation of God the Son, referred to as "the face of the Lord" or "the presence of the Lord."[13] While the Father cannot be seen, there is a "face to face" Lord to whom Moses speaks *as a friend*. It is this person who, the Father promises, will go with Moses as the guarantee of his favor: "My presence [literally, "my face"] will go with you, and I will give you rest" (v. 14). Without him, Moses knows he cannot go. "If your presence ["face"] will not go with me, do not bring us up from here" (v. 15). Isaiah 63:9 will speak of him as "the angel of his presence ["face"],"[14] and so it is that Paul can write that God has "shone in our hearts to give the light of the knowledge of the glory of God in the *face* of Jesus Christ" (2 Cor. 4:6). The Son is the one who will take responsibility for Moses and the Israelites. He will be to them the face of God, the name of God, and the Glory of God, dwelling among them in his own holy tent wherever they go, always revealing, leading, and protecting them in his Father's ways. He is the one who will finally lead them into their rest in the promised land (Ex. 33:14).

The blessing that the Lord gives to Moses and Aaron to bless the people of Israel opens up his desire in all this:

The LORD bless you and keep you;
the LORD make his *face to shine upon you* and be gracious to you;
the LORD lift up his countenance upon you and give you peace.
    (Num. 6:24–26)

---

13 Edwards, *Works*, 21:375–76.
14 This in no way implies that the Son is an angelic creature of some kind. The Hebrew word translated "angel," מַלְאָךְ (*malak*), simply means "messenger" or "sent one."

Notice that this is not a prayer that Moses and Aaron imaginatively invent. These are the words given to them by the Lord so that, he says, they may "*put my name* upon the people of Israel, and I will bless them" (Num. 6:27). God's own words, lent to the mouths of the priests of Israel to pray back to him, declare that *by the glorious beams of his face and presence* his treasured people would receive his blessing, grace, and peace.

Today, when we speak about "the presence of God," we can tend to be quite abstract, perhaps mentioning in passing that we gather at church "in the presence of God." Others speak about "sensing the presence of God" in worship or prayer. We can be a little vague, too, about the "glory of God," thinking generally about God's majesty and power, and the way the wonders of creation seem to reflect something of him. Some Christians claim to have seen "glory clouds" or felt the "weight of glory" in a place. But what we have seen in Scripture guides us to a much more specific and significant understanding of these things. God's presence, name, face, and glory are all in a *person*. Jesus Christ *is* in himself the radiant display of the reality of God. Moreover, he is to us the gift of God's *very self*.

A Vast Love unto Us

Jesus is God shining, going out from the Father in radiant revelation to give himself to us. He is God's face turned toward us, God's name dwelling with us, and God's glory flashing upon us. Jesus shows us a God who is fundamentally outgoing, outshining, and self-giving. He wants to be known by us, to be with us, even possessed by us, so that we will call him *our* God (Jer. 31:33). To accomplish this, he takes the initiative himself. This is precisely what we see in the Son's incarnation.

While we had sinned against him and rejected him, he "left His Father's throne above, / So free, so infinite His grace," as Charles Wesley had it.[15] Taking our humanity upon himself and stepping into the world, he came *out* to "seek and save the lost" (Luke 19:10), going about from town to town searching for the broken, tormented, and dying, to heal and raise them up. Moving to the fringes of society and further, he reached out to lepers, prostitutes, tax collectors, and sinners. The good shepherd would leave the fold for even one of his flock in danger (Luke 15:4). Stretching beyond only the lost sheep of the house of Israel, he beamed on Samaritans, Romans, and Canaanites (Matt. 15:21–28). In the end, his purpose was to draw all people to himself (John 12:32). His journey outward was also a journey *downward*. In humility, he took "the form of a servant" (Phil. 2:7), stooped to wash the feet of disciples, and explained that "the Son of Man came not to be served but to serve" (Mark 10:45).

In Jesus's beautiful life—the most beautiful life ever lived—God's own face shines on us. This is what it is to have *God with us*, Immanuel. The one in whom "the whole fullness of deity dwells bodily" (Col. 2:9) "became flesh and dwelt among us, and we have seen his glory, glory as of the only Son *from the Father*, full of grace and truth" (John 1:14). This is the one who is the "radiance of the glory of God," and if these are the beams, then such is the great Sun that emits them. Jesus himself could not be clearer in saying that he only ever does what he sees his Father doing (John 5:19) and that if we have seen him, then we have seen the Father (John 14:9). It is this most kind, compassionate, and unselfish one that the Father speaks

---

15 Charles Wesley, "And Can It Be That I Should Gain" (1738), https://hymnary.org.

about as his "chosen one" and the delight of his soul in Isaiah 42:1. He who will not break a bruised reed or snuff out a flickering wick is the one the Father uniquely endorses and approves.

> I am the LORD; that is my name;
> *my glory I give to no other.* (Isa. 42:8)

> This is my beloved Son, with whom I am well pleased. (Matt. 3:17)

There could be no stronger indication from God that what we see in his Son is flawlessly like him and exactly what most pleases and expresses his own heart.

Thomas Goodwin knew how hard it was for us to take this in. He wrote that we more easily imagine that God forgives and blesses us not because of his care for us or any movement in his own heart toward us but simply because he grants Jesus's request, made on our behalf. It is a dark thought many of us have entertained, driving a wedge between a benevolent Jesus and a harsher Father. Goodwin corrects us:

> *You are deceived,* says Christ, *it is otherwise; my Father's heart is as much towards you, and for your salvation, as mine is; himself, of himself, loves you.* And the truth is, that God took up as vast a love unto us of himself at first as ever he has borne us since, and all that Christ does for us is but the expression of that love which was taken up originally in God's own heart. Thus we find that out of that love he gave Christ for us. . . . Christ adds not one drop of love to God's heart, only draws it out; he broaches it, and makes it flow forth.[16]

---

16 Thomas Goodwin, *The Works of Thomas Goodwin*, vol. 4, *Christ Set Forth* (Edinburgh: Nichol, 1862), 87.

Jesus is the outshining, overflowing, loving largesse of God the Father. And it is the Father's good pleasure to give him to us (Luke 12:32).

Mission's Motor

If someone were to ask us, "What is God like?" the answer must be "Jesus Christ." That is the result of all we have seen about the glory of God. Bound up in all this is the fact that the very being of God is outwardly propulsive. God, in having glory, *radiates*; in having a Word, *speaks*; in having a Son, *loves*. It is his very nature to shine, communicate, and give himself in relationship. This is the beating heart of mission.

The glory of God is often rightly spoken of as the *goal* and *end point* of mission. The Westminster Shorter Catechism famously says, "Man's chief end is to *glorify* God, and to enjoy him forever."[17] The missionary efforts of the church are the means to the end that our God is worshiped by all the people of the earth. The desires of a growing Christian come to align with God's own, and it becomes our cherished concern that God is seen and known for who he truly is.

Yet God's glory is not only the fuel of mission in the sense of being its grand objective. God's glory—his own naturally overspilling life, showcased in his Son—is mission's *rationale* and its motor. In whatever sense mission is about our going out into the world to make God known, it is only ever our being caught up in the already gushing tide of blessing that flows from the heart of the Father in the Son. Charles Spurgeon said, "When I think of God I am led to

---

17 Question 1 (emphasis added).

see his glory in the outgoing of his great heart; for he is altogether unselfish and unsparingly communicative."[18]

Those who bask in the sunshine of this loving and generous God are the happiest Christians and the happiest missionaries. Set free from an impoverished view of God—a god we could not truly enjoy or willingly serve—we now know ourselves loved unconditionally and beyond measure, and love God in return. Seeing in Jesus what our God is really like causes us to shine like him. We come to share his great heart's desire that his love, goodness, and righteousness would bless all the world.

But we haven't said all that must be said about the glory of God. We haven't yet said everything that must be said about Jesus. There is a strange but brighter brightness we still need to unveil: his death for us.

18 C. H. Spurgeon, "The Glory of God in the Face of Jesus Christ" (September 7, 1879), in *The Metropolitan Tabernacle Pulpit*, vol. 25 (London: Passmore & Alabaster, 1879), 510.

2

The Lamb on His Throne

CHRISTIANS SPEAK QUITE A BIT about God's glory, but we don't always do so in a thoroughly *Christian* way. We may acknowledge that Christ is the Glory of God and speak about him, but we haven't plumbed the definition of the word *glory*. We treat it as though its meaning were self-evident and self-explanatory, allowing our natural, human idea of glory to lead the charge in our imaginations. In our fallen thinking, for God to be glorious is simply for him to be *great*. Of course, this is the sort of glory we would quite like for ourselves: we want to be recognized, given credit, and known for our skills and abilities. We want to be praised and pumped up, and our pursuit of this glory might lead to competition (subtle or not) with siblings, colleagues, or friends. At times, it can bring out the very worst in us. We reason that God, being God, really *is* the center of the universe, so he has and deserves glory to the highest degree. But, while God has no serious competition for his glory, we read into God's glory the same kind of standoffishness and self-centeredness that tends to course through our own.

The great danger here is a theology of glory that hasn't passed through the prism of the gospel of Jesus. We risk projecting our own darkness and selfishness onto the living God, making him far less good and beautiful than he really is. This will always be the result of starting out with our own assumptions rather than his word to us. When we begin to see Jesus as himself the Glory of the Father and let him shape our idea of glory, we find that God is far better than we ever dared to believe, and his glory, beautifully different from our own. Nowhere is this more sharply detailed—and nowhere is the glory of God more tightly defined in Scripture—than on the cross of Jesus.

In the Throne Room

In the book of Revelation, the apostle John has a glimpse behind the curtain of the cosmos. As he looks into the great spiritual realities of the heavenly realm, he sees a throne (4:3). The throne is center stage in a scene of almost indescribable glory: the sparkle of precious stones, a rainbow of color, golden crowns, thunder and lightning, burning torches, mighty angels, praising saints, and the living God seated amid it all. In his hand is a sealed scroll (5:1) that, we learn through the book, contains the meaning of history and the great arc of the purposes of God in it all. Nobody in heaven or on earth is found who can open the scroll and unlock the mysteries within. Nobody, that is, until John is told that there is one who has conquered and who is worthy to take it: the Lion of the Tribe of Judah (5:5). Of course! The royal tribe (long associated with lions, Gen. 49:9) finds in the king of beasts triumphant power. What better pedigree for the one to step up to the throne? "Cometh the hour, cometh the man!" the saying goes. But as John watches and the conqueror appears, he sees not a roaring lion, but "a Lamb standing, as though it had been slain" (Rev. 5:6). The Lamb takes the scroll and opens the seals, and the company of heaven sings to him,

Worthy are you to take the scroll
    and to open its seals,
for you were slain, and by your blood you ransomed people
        for God
    from every tribe and language and people and nation.
    (Rev. 5:9)

John is not unfamiliar with the sight of slaughtered lambs from his visits to the Jerusalem temple. He has seen the exposed innards, the bloodied wool, and the limp, lifeless limbs. A sacrificial victim is not the hero he was expecting to appear in that celestial throne room. Now, the Lamb is not dead—he is standing, resurrected—but the marks of his death are visible, and the fruit of his death is the theme of heaven's song. As John's vision continues, that theme remains as this Lamb mounts the throne (Rev. 7:17) where, finally, he is married in rejoicing and exultation (Rev. 19:7).

Here is the most surprising and counterintuitive message. We would never have expected the God of glory to be revealed *this* way: in death. We might well have imagined that the interpretive key to history and the guide to all its true meaning and significance is Christ, the Lamb. Yet this is specifically *the Lamb who was slain.* The rise and fall of empires, all political intrigue and power plays, all fame and fortune, tragedy and triumph, all the trials and suffering of the people of God from Adam to the present day are all summed up and put in their proper place by the slain Lamb. To the suffering and persecuted churches first receiving John's book, this must have been a startling and heartening dose of reality.

It must be the same for us today. Only with our eyes on Christ crucified do we see the truth, perspective, and logic of all the providence of God in everything that has happened since the beginning.

Only with our eyes on Christ crucified do we see who our God really and truly is.

The Light Shines from the Cross

While we generally think of the cross of Christ in terms of the atonement and its saving purpose, there is also an element of *revelation* to it. The death of Jesus, in all its redeeming power, also shows us the truth about God, us, and everything. As much as darkness fell as God's judgment was meted out at Calvary, from the cross a light shines on every other event and person in history, every doctrine, and every passage of Scripture.

> In the cross of Christ I glory,
>   towering o'er the wrecks of time;
> all the light of sacred story
>   gathers round its head sublime.[1]

Paul writes that the cross is the point at which God slices into our human ways of thinking—so thoroughly distorted and polluted by sin—to confront us and contradict us. Our natural assumption is that the crucifixion of the Son of God would be "folly" (1 Cor. 1:18), when in fact it is "the power of God and the wisdom of God" displayed (1 Cor. 1:24). A crucified Messiah is a stumbling block to any who would look for miraculous signs or profound wisdom as the sure signs of divinity at work, but Paul makes it the very heart of his message (1 Cor. 1:22–23; 2:2). In this way, the cross of Jesus stands in judgment over all human wisdom, power, and boasting, "so that, as it is written, 'Let the one who boasts, boast in the Lord'"

---

1 John Bowring, "In the Cross of Christ I Glory" (1825), https://hymnary.org.

(1 Cor. 1:31). If we want to know the true power and wisdom of God, then it is to the cross we must look.

Seeing all this, Martin Luther was known to say, "The cross alone is our theology," and so "the cross tests everything."[2] The cross, he saw, was to be the compass, the litmus test, and the quality control mechanism for all our thinking about God. There are, says Luther, two roads when it comes to thinking about God.[3] The first is a "theology of glory." He has in mind here that very human idea of glory as greatness and self-promotion. Someone doing theology this way considers himself able to turn to God of his own free will, and so would trust in his own good works, believing that his efforts must surely be impressive. Misusing the law of God, he would consider it a ladder to advance his own (presumed) righteousness, "without fear and in unadulterated, evil self-security."[4] This theologian, Luther says, is "completely puffed up, blinded, and hardened," for the theology of glory finally "calls evil good and good evil."[5] It fatally misunderstands the human predicament, the nature of salvation, and God himself. Relying on himself, this kind of theologian looks to *earn* glory from God.

The cross turns this kind of thinking upside down. On the cross, we see God's verdict on all human efforts to know and please God: they are condemned in the flesh of Christ (Rom. 8:3). The punishment of the cross is all we deserve. As Jesus bears the punishment

---

2 Martin Luther, *Luther's Commentary on the First Twenty-Two Psalms*, trans. J. N. Lenker, vol. 1 (Sunbury, PA: Lutherans in All Lands, 1903), 289, 294–95.

3 Martin Luther, "Heidelberg Disputation, 1518," in *Luther's Works*, vol. 31, *Career of the Reformer I*, ed. Harold J. Grimm and Helmut T. Lehmann (Philadelphia: Fortress; St. Louis, MO: Concordia, 1957), 36ff.

4 Luther, *Works*, 31:40.

5 Luther, *Works*, 31:40.

that was due to us, our true nature is brought into the light: we are helpless sinners, and the nails are driven thorough all our pride and self-sufficiency. Like the bright white light above your bathroom mirror, the cross uncovers every imperfection and flaw we have tried to mask. Our constant bent toward evil is laid bare, and all the goodness we have foolishly boasted in is exposed as sin layered upon sin. The law we once thought was our surefire way to glory actually "kills, reviles, accuses, judges, and condemns everything that is not in Christ."[6] At the cross, the proud must hang their heads, because it disqualifies all of us from standing before God on our own merit. Nothing in us and nothing we can bring to God can ever make us right with him or impress him.

From this profound despair at our own inability, the second road opens up: a "theology of the cross." This theology sees things as they really are, comprehending the things of God *through suffering and the cross.*[7] Hidden in the appalling spectacle of the crucifixion, which appears "unattractive and evil," is the beautiful work of God.[8] At the cross, God graciously gives himself for us and to be known by us, entirely without our contribution, which now reeks to us (Isa. 64:6). God himself has intervened in the world to show us himself and to save us for himself. As our own efforts to know and impress God are crucified with Christ, legalistic shoulders may relax, and self-despairing sinners may heave a sigh of relief. All our fevered reputation management, comparison with other Christians, and guilty fears about what really lurks beneath the veneer are swept away from us. Truly, we have always been hopeless and helpless if not for Christ, and so we

6 Luther, *Works*, 31:41.
7 Luther, *Works*, 31:40.
8 Luther, *Works*, 31:39.

gratefully collapse into him. "He is not righteous who does much,"
Luther writes, "but he who, without work, believes much in Christ."
Here we find that, while the law says, "'Do this,' and it is never done,"
God's grace says, "'Believe in this,' and everything is already done."[9]

At the heart of Luther's view of revelation and salvation is the fact
that "the love of God does not *find* but *creates* that which is pleasing
to it."[10] In his love, God *gives to us* what we need to know him and
have fellowship with him. It is all by his grace and does not rely on
us in any way. Doing theology from the cross is like going through
the looking glass with Alice into a totally different way of seeing everything. In fact, it is a death-and-resurrection experience for us, as
"the LORD kills and brings to life" (1 Sam. 2:6). The air on the other
side is different, and there is a freshness and beauty that we never
sensed before. God truly *loves* us sinners and has done everything
necessary to redeem us and bring us to himself. He is not interested
in our intelligence, morality, or abilities so much as our loving trust
and reliance on him in his goodness. This is the revelation of the
cross and the sunshine it pours into our lives.

The Cross in the Heart of God

We are not being negative about the glory *of God* here. Luther has
been taking aim specifically at the kind of glory that selfish sinners
would imagine and want for themselves.[11] He is not setting God's true
glory and the cross at odds with one another, as though God can be
glorious *or* he can be self-giving, depending on his mood.

---

9   Luther, *Works*, 31:41.
10 Luther, *Works*, 31:41.
11 Christopher Jackson, "Luther's Theologian of the Cross and Theologian of Glory Distinction
    Reconsidered," *Pro Ecclesia* 29, no. 3 (2020): 1–16. Jackson points out that "a thorough-going
    theology of glory is crucial for Christian discipleship" and that Luther clearly has one. See chap. 6.

So how are we to relate the glory of God to the cross? If Christ is the radiance of God's glory, is the crucifixion not the Glory of God himself being snuffed out? Is his resurrection his reversion back to being glorious and divine after a short time in ignominy and disgrace? This is an important pastoral question, because many of us see the grace and mercy on display in Jesus's death for us but fear it was nothing more than an episode of atypical friendliness in God. We are grateful beyond words for his salvation but sense that once the cross is over and done with, the next chapter begins, and God returns to being majestically severe. The self-giving of Christ in his death had to take place to achieve our salvation, but we darkly doubt that, in himself, God is really very much like *that*.

Scripture says much to comfort us here. Peter's Pentecost sermon sees the root of the crucifixion in "the definite plan and foreknowledge of God" (Acts 2:23), and Ephesians 1 places the plan for our redemption in Christ "before the foundation of the world" and God's "plan for the fullness of time" (vv. 3–10). In Philippians 2, Paul paints a picture of the Son in eternity considering his own divinity and equality with God and counting it something not to be "grasped," or held on to for his own advantage, but rather choosing to pour himself out in humility even unto death on the cross (vv. 5–11). The cross is clearly no whim or fly-by-night escapade. Christ Jesus, in the eternal will of the Father, considered his death the very exercise of his deity.

There is more. On top of all this, John's Gospel speaks of Jesus's death *as his glory*.

Blood and Glory

In John 2, Jesus attends the wedding in Cana where the wine runs out. When his mother, Mary, asks him to step in and help, he puzzlingly replies, "My hour has not yet come" (v. 4). Nevertheless, he turns water into wine, to the delight of the wedding guests, and John notes, "This, the first of his signs, Jesus did at Cana in Galilee, and manifested his glory" (v. 11). This sets up questions that hang over the rest of his Gospel. When will be the "hour" or moment to which Jesus is referring? What is the "glory" he is manifesting (which John says he has seen in John 1:14)?

As the chapters roll on, Jesus continues to look forward to an "hour" that is yet to come (John 4:23; 5:25, 28; 7:30; 8:20) and values only the glory of God rather than that of man (John 5:41, 44; 7:18; 8:50, 54). Then, in John 12, Jesus enters the city of Jerusalem, and everything falls into place at once. Jesus says to Andrew and Philip that, at long last, "the hour has come for the Son of Man to be glorified" (v. 23). This, he likens to a grain of wheat falling to the earth and dying in order to bear much fruit (vv. 24–25). Then comes one of the most remarkable events recorded in the Gospel as Jesus prays to his Father.

> "Now is my soul troubled. And what shall I say? 'Father, save me from this hour'? But for this purpose I have come to this hour. Father, glorify your name." Then a voice came from heaven: "I have glorified it, and I will glorify it again." The crowd that stood there and heard it said that it had thundered. Others said, "An angel has spoken to him." Jesus answered, "This voice has come for your sake, not mine. Now is the judgment of this world; now will the ruler of this world be cast out. And I, when I am lifted up from the earth, will draw all people to myself." He said this to show by what kind of death he was going to die. (vv. 27–33)

The hour of Jesus's glorification is nothing other than the soul-troubling death that lies before him. The glory—the weight and substance of *who he is*—will be set out for all to see on the cross. This was his purpose from the beginning, and not only his glorification but the Father's glorification *in him.* Jesus considers the "hour" in which he is hoisted up in shame and agony on the tree to be the moment of his glory and of his Father's great pleasure in him. In John 17:24, just hours before he goes to his death, Jesus asks his Father that all Christians would, he prays, "see my glory that you have given me because you loved me before the foundation of the world." Could it be that, in the horror of Golgotha, we see played out before us the *love and glory* of the Father and Son? That God shows us most deeply and wonderfully who he is in this sacrifice of himself?

Cyril of Alexandria comments on this chapter:

> The cross is glory. Indeed, at the time of suffering, he patiently and willingly endured many insults that he did not have to suffer. He subjected himself to suffering willingly for us, and undergoing this for the benefit of others is a mark of extreme compassion and the highest glory. . . . The Father is glorified when he shows that he has a Son who is *like he is.* . . . After all, the Father did not give the Son over to death without thinking about it, but *intentionally for the life of the world.*[12]

The Roman soldiers cannot have known the truth they were preaching as they mockingly laid on him the purple robe and crown of thorns, fixing to his cross the sign "the King of the Jews." For here was the King of the universe bearing in himself all the curse (Gen. 3:18); the Lamb taking up his throne. Against all our fears, the cross was not a detour for God the Son. It was and is his glory. It is his

---

12 Cyril of Alexandria, *Commentary on John*, vol. 2, trans. David R. Maxwell, ed. Joel C. Elowsky, Ancient Christian Texts (Downers Grove, IL: InterVarsity Press, 2015), 106 (emphasis added).

glory that his soul should be troubled so that ours need not be (John 12:27; 14:1), that he himself should go down into the grave to bear the fruit of our eternal life (John 12:24), that he should be crucified between two thieves, "numbered with the transgressors" (Isa. 53:12), in the fate that should have been ours. As the eternal one empties himself into history and his love is poured out in blood, just as the festal wine has been, we can only stand amazed and say, with Thomas, "My Lord and my God!" (John 20:28).

Lifted Up to Shine on Us

The prophet Isaiah foresaw all of this. On the day he was called to prophetic ministry, he had a dramatic vision. "I saw the Lord sitting upon a throne, high and lifted up; and the train of his robe filled the temple" (6:1). The very foundations of the temple shook, and smoke filled the house as the seraphim cried,

> Holy, holy, holy is the LORD of hosts;
> the whole earth is full of his glory! (6:3–4)

The idea of someone "high and lifted up" on a throne conjures in our minds an ancient monarch driven around in a litter—or perhaps a sports star, having scored the winning goal or hit a walk-off home run, carried on the shoulders of adoring teammates. He or she is the center of attention, soaking up the adulation, perhaps proudly self-satisfied. Such is human glory. But the next time Isaiah uses the phrase "high and lifted up," it is at the end of chapter 52, where we read:

> Behold, my servant shall act wisely;
> he shall be *high and lifted up*,
> and shall be *exalted*.
> As many were astonished at you—

his appearance was so marred, beyond human semblance,
and his form beyond that of the children of mankind.
(vv. 13–14)

And in chapter 53, we read:

He was pierced for our transgressions;
he was crushed for our iniquities;
upon him was the chastisement that brought us peace,
and with his wounds we are healed.
All we like sheep have gone astray;
we have turned—every one—to his own way;
and the LORD has laid on him
the iniquity of us all. (vv. 5–6)

Isaiah said these things, John writes (John 12:41), because he saw
Jesus's glory and spoke of him. Jesus explained that his "lifted up"
death had a special significance in that he was *seen*. He compared it
to the day in Numbers 21:4–9 when fiery serpents were killing the
people of Israel, and Moses raised a bronze serpent on a pole. Anyone
who was bitten could simply look to the uplifted serpent and live.
"And as Moses lifted up the serpent in the wilderness," said Jesus, "so
must the Son of Man be lifted up, that whoever believes in him may
have eternal life" (John 3:14). Jesus's being "lifted up" and "exalted"
is about his salvation being seen to be believed. It is broadcast and
trumpeted, "put forward" (Rom. 3:25), and "publicly portrayed"
(Gal. 3:1) that we might look upon him and live.

Another Old Testament prophet to have a vision of the Lord gloriously enthroned was Ezekiel. One day by Babylon's Chebar Canal,
he saw the same dazzling scene that John would later: a great cloud
with the flashings of fire, living creatures, and the great throne.

Seated on the throne was "a likeness with a human appearance" with brightness all around him (Ezek. 1:26–27). Ezekiel strained to describe what he saw:

> Like the appearance of the bow that is in the cloud on the day of rain, so was the appearance of the brightness all around.
>
> Such was the appearance of the likeness of the glory of the Lord. And when I saw it, I fell on my face, and I heard the voice of one speaking. (1:28)

John's vision of the Lamb enthroned was also marked by the appearance of a rainbow (Rev. 4:3). This sign the Lord had first put in the sky after the flood. It was to be a reminder to Noah and to all creation that God would never again judge the earth by destroying all life with a flood. The Lord even speaks of the rainbow as a reminder to himself of this eternal covenant and promise (Gen. 9:11–16). The "bow" in the clouds is a bow for arrows; for hunting or for battle (Gen. 48:22; 2 Chron. 18:33). The sign from the Lord that he will never again destroy all flesh is his own war bow set in the clouds, armed and aimed at heaven. The Lord's everlasting covenant was fulfilled when the Son took upon himself the flood of judgment on our sin. This is the light that encircles the very throne of heaven. Comparing the throne to the ark in the tabernacle, Jonathan Edwards writes, "God is encompassed with a rainbow, which signifies that as he sits, and reigns, and manifests himself in his church, he appears as encompassed with mercy."[13]

When Jesus, himself the Glory of God, was lifted up on the cross, it was no fireworks display for his own amusement; no yelling in an

---

13 Jonathan Edwards, *The Works of Jonathan Edwards*, vol. 15, *Notes on Scripture*, ed. Stephen J. Stein (New Haven, CT: Yale University Press, 1998), 224.

empty room. It was a real explosion of God's mercy into our midnight. It was a rainbow of color splashed across the dark Babylonian sky. It was the goodness, light, and life of God penetrating the evil, shadow, and death of our sin so that we might look and live. It was the light shining on the land of deep darkness (Isa. 9:2), the sunrise from on high (Luke 1:78), the dawning of the "sun of righteousness" with his healing wings (Mal. 4:2). The Son was lifted up to bestow blessing and life on the world. At the cross, God was giving himself to us. There we see God going, reaching, and *shining* out.

Out of Zion, the Perfection of Beauty

The location of Jesus's death outside the city wall of Jerusalem was no accident. From the beginning, Jerusalem was the place where the Lord shone his light. King David's capital was built on Mount Zion (2 Sam. 5:7), which had been instrumental for Abraham and many others, and was sometimes known as Moriah (Gen. 22:2; 2 Chron. 3:1). It was home to the temple, where the Lord dwelt among his people, just as he had in the tabernacle in the wilderness (1 Kings 8:1–13). Because God was in the midst of the city, it would not be moved (Ps. 46:5).

It was to Jerusalem, year after year, that pilgrims would go up to keep the feasts of the Lord, pray in the temple, and seek the face of God. On this mountain, Abraham had prepared to sacrifice his son, Isaac, but instead prophesied, "God will provide for himself the lamb" (Gen. 22:8). After sacrificing an adult ram rather than his boy, Abraham called that place "'The LORD will provide'; as it is said to this day, 'On the mount of the LORD *it shall be provided*'" (Gen. 22:14). In addition, the Lord had said to Isaiah that he would put his salvation "in Zion, / for Israel my glory" (Isa. 46:13), and the psalmist had cried out, "Oh, that salvation for Israel would come out of Zion!" (Ps. 14:7). So, to this mountain city, through the generations, lambs were brought to die. Each spring as the Passover feast marked the redemption of the Israelites from slavery in Egypt, thousands of lambs would be herded into the city, kept there for four days, then slain in the temple (Ex. 12:3, 6; Deut. 16:5–6). *The* Lamb was coming.

When the Lord visited the temple as a boy, it was not his first time there. On that same mountain, he had dwelt in the Most Holy Place, enthroned in his glory above the cherubim on the ark of the covenant. He had seen the generations of high priests entering behind the curtain on the Day of Atonement, watched the blood sprinkled on the mercy seat, and seen his people represented as precious stones over the heart of the Levite (Ex. 28:15–30). He had heard as the people outside celebrated when the high priest reemerged with atonement completed, and he had always known that his hour would soon come. And so, it was to Jerusalem, four days before his crucifixion, that the Lamb of God made his way (Luke 9:51).

God Shines Forth

The writer to the Hebrews tells us that when Christ presented himself as the great high priest and the once-for-all sacrifice to end all sacrifices, he passed through not the *earthly* tent, for this was only ever a copy of the true *heavenly* throne room (8:1–6). No, "for Christ has entered, not into holy places made with hands, which are copies of the true things, but into heaven itself, now to appear in the presence of God on our behalf" (9:24). Jesus's work on the cross in the earthly Zion that day was the throwing open of the gates that had been shut: the way to face-to-face fellowship with God for all who would come—citizenship in the heavenly Zion where God and the Lamb are surrounded by the saints and angels.

You have come to Mount Zion and to the city of the living God, the heavenly Jerusalem, and to innumerable angels in festal gathering, and to the assembly of the firstborn who are enrolled in heaven, and to God, the judge of all, and to the spirits of the righteous made perfect, and to Jesus, the mediator of a new covenant. (12:22–24)

On the day of that once-for-all offering, Jerusalem below, after years in prophetic expectation, became the pathway to the "Jerusalem above" (Gal. 4:26). It is no wonder that Zion was always pictured as a place of outstanding beauty that beamed with the salvation and glory of the Lord. Her brilliance and perfection seemed to come from elsewhere; she shone with a unique, otherworldly beauty that made her the talk of all the nations.

> Great is the LORD and greatly to be praised
>   in the city of our God!
> His holy mountain, beautiful in elevation,
>   is the joy of all the earth,
> Mount Zion, in the far north,
>   the city of the great King.
> Within its citadels God
>   has made himself known as a fortress. (Ps. 48:1–3)

> The Mighty One, God the LORD,
>   speaks and summons the earth
>   from the rising of the sun to its setting.
> *Out of Zion, the perfection of beauty,*
>   *God shines forth.* (Ps. 50:1–2)

> Glorious things of you are spoken,
>   O city of God. (Ps. 87:3)

Where the Lord was present with his people, his very own light and life shone out. This was never so true as on Good Friday when the Glory of God was lifted up on his throne for the blessing of the world. From Zion—the mountain of God, the Most Holy Place, the cross of Christ—God shines forth. His love and life are a streaming fountain of mercy, gladness, and treasure. Even desert places and barren hearts bud and flourish as this God is seen for who he truly is. Joyful singing and smiles of pleasure are sure to erupt where he shows his face. At the cross, God shows himself to be fruitful and life-giving—even in the face of death and sin. That is, he shows himself *glorious*.

Who Is Like the Lord Our God?

The cross is glory in that God shows himself there decisively. The cross is the glorification of *the* Glory (the Son!) of God. It stands as the defining moment in God's relationship to all creation—the pinnacle and epitome of all he desires to show us of himself. It is a self-assertion and a self-declaration, but one that is less like a political manifesto and more like a proposal of marriage. God says to his people at the cross of Jesus: "*This* is who I am. All that I am I give to you, and all that I have I share with you."

The revelation of God at the cross torpedoes our expectations of him. Where we have imagined him to be distant and severe, the cross says, "God so loved the world, that he gave his only Son" (John 3:16). Where we have imagined him demanding a perfection we cannot offer, the cross says, "God shows his love for us in that while we were still sinners, Christ died for us" (Rom. 5:8). Where we have imagined ourselves dropping out of God's favor by our frequent disobedience, the cross says: "If anyone does sin, we have an advocate with the Father, Jesus Christ the righteous. He is the propitiation for our sins" (1 John 2:1–2). This way, the cross kindly puts us to death, contradicting us in every way, totally upending our human ways of thinking. All this is completely beautiful to us as we sing with the psalmist,

> Who is like the LORD our God,
>   who is seated on high,
> who looks far down
>   on the heavens and the earth? (Ps. 113:5–6)

3

Fullness

No question is more important than this one. It is a matter of life and death that Jesus truly shows us his Father. The gospel, our mission, and our eternal life depend on there being no different God "backstage" of the manger and the cross; that the kind of glory on display in the Son shows who God is *all the way down*. If Jesus is not the definitive word on the nature of God, then some other god lurks behind him. But if Jesus truly is the radiance of the Father, then all the goodness we see demonstrated and enacted in Christ's living, dying, and rising flows from God's own eternal life and being.

What is the source of the breathtaking goodness we see in the incarnation and cross of Christ? What kind of God would behave in such a way toward sinners?

I Am Who I Am

In Exodus 3, Moses meets the Lord at the burning bush and asks him, "What is your name?" The Lord answers, "I AM WHO I AM. . . . Say this to the people of Israel: 'I AM has sent me to you'" (v. 14). God has answered Moses with a sentence. But then he says, "*The* LORD, the God of your fathers, the God of Abraham, the God of Isaac, and the

God of Jacob, has sent me to you" (v. 15). These two parallel answers are related. The name "Lord" in our Bibles stands in for the name יהוה (*YHWH*), which, in turn, comes from the word for "I am." It is the name Jesus uses in John's Gospel when he proclaims, "Before Abraham was, *I am*" (John 8:58). When we speak of "the Lord," we are, in effect, calling God "the One Who Is," for he does not receive his name, identity, or existence from anyone or anything else: the life of God is self-contained and self-sustaining. He does not depend on anything to be who he is: he simply and eternally *is*.

This is the doctrine of God's self-existence, or *aseity* (from the Latin *a se*, "from/of himself"). Unlike us, the Lord is not contingent upon anyone or anything. He is who he is in and of himself, having his life and being independently, completely, and eternally. This is a truth we meet again and again throughout Scripture. We read, "In the beginning, God . . ." (Gen. 1:1) because he was there before all things. Moses prayed, "From everlasting to everlasting you are God" (Ps. 90:2) because his very way of being transcends all history. Indeed, Jesus calls himself "the Alpha and the Omega, the first and the last, the beginning and the end" (Rev. 22:13). One of the Lord's titles is the *living* God (Deut. 5:26; Dan. 6:26), and David writes of the Lord, "With you is the fountain of life" (Ps. 36:9), because God is so full of life.

Just as God does not rely on anything outside himself, so also within himself he does not have any parts or components he depends on in order to be who he is. He is "simple." No quality or idea or thing preexists him from which he could derive his being. No feature or attribute of his comes from before him or outside him. For example, God does not *have* something called "love" that exists in some way independent of him—a quality or activity he could acquire. No, God *is* love in the fellowship of Father, Son, and Holy Spirit. You couldn't remove God's love from him as we might remove an appendix or snip off our hair, for love isn't a *part* of God, but *is* who he is. And so it is for all of him: his goodness, truth, beauty, holiness. Because he is simple, he doesn't depend on anything to be himself—not even his own characteristics and qualities.

This means that God's attributes are not in any kind of competition or delicate balance within him. You will have heard Christians say, "Yes, God is loving, but he is *also* wrathful." In one sense this is correct, but it can give the impression that God is sometimes in a loving mood and sometimes in a wrathful mood and that, when he's feeling one, he's not feeling the other. But these are not separate *parts* of God: they actually belong together. God is angry at evil *because* he loves and because there is no evil in his eternal life. His wrath proves the sincerity and potency of his love, showing us that he truly *cares* about goodness! Most deeply of all, God's simplicity means that his being Father to the Son is not something additional to his being, nor something superficial. He is eternally Father and fatherly.

In his self-existent perfection, our God does not evolve or improve. Having fullness of being, how could he? He is "immutable," meaning that he does not require anything in order to be "better," to be "more God," or to be more fully "himself." In him there is no fickleness, there are no mood swings or fads, so that "the Glory of Israel will not lie or have regret, for he is not a man, that he should have regret" (1 Sam. 15:29). James writes of "the Father of lights, with whom there is no variation or shadow due to change" (1:17). God does not "become"—there is no moment when the Father *becomes* a father, or the Son a son. There was no loneliness in the Father, that he had to go out and find a Son. God's eternal life is unbeatably perfect as it is.

No wonder David could pray: "Therefore you are great, O LORD God. For *there is none like you, and there is no God besides you*" (2 Sam. 7:22), and the psalmist could write,

> For you, O LORD, are most high over all the earth;
> you are exalted far above all gods. (Ps. 97:9)

Great and exalted, the living God stands apart from us and over us and has no need of us! As Paul tells the Athenians, "The God who made the world and everything in it, being Lord of heaven and earth, does not live in temples made by man, nor is he served by human hands, *as though he needed anything*" (Acts 17:24–25).

No, the triune God who made the world isn't in any need. He depends on nothing. He has fullness of being, life eternal and unfaltering in himself. Far from being needy, our God is the very definition of fullness. God alone is gloriously, completely, independently himself. This is God—Father, Son, and Spirit—before, beyond, and above all created things. Yet the triune life is not a fortress, shut up against the world. God's satisfied self-existence does not mean grand isolation, vacuum-packed and hidden away. No, the very life of God—all that he is in himself—overflows.

The Infinite Happiness of God

Jesus the Son is the radiance of the glory of God (Heb. 1:3), and as we follow the beams back to their source and gaze into the very being of the Lord, we discover a fundamentally *giving, loving* kind of God.

God the Father has eternally given to his Son. "For as the Father has life in himself," Jesus says, "so he has granted the Son also to have life in himself" (John 5:26). This life giving or "begetting" has no start point, for the Son "was *in the beginning with God*" (John 1:2); neither is the Son someone other than God, because "the Word *was* God" in the beginning (John 1:1). The Father and Son are one being, one God, sharing the same life. The eternal life of God *is* the Father begetting his Son in the Holy Spirit. The nature and quality of this eternal life is revealed to us when, on the night of his arrest, Jesus prays, "Father . . . you *loved* me before the foundation of the world" (John 17:24). In expression of this love, the Father entrusts all his works to the Son: "The Father loves the Son and has given all things into his hand" (John 3:35). The Spirit, who is always the bringer of unity and fellowship (2 Cor. 13:14; Eph. 4:3), carries and embodies this love, so that Luke can tell us that Jesus

> *rejoiced in the Holy Spirit* and said, "I thank you, Father, Lord of heaven and earth, that you have hidden these things from the wise and understanding and revealed them to little children; yes, Father, for such was your gracious will. All things have been handed over to me by my Father and no one knows who the Son is except the Father, or who the Father is except the Son and anyone to whom the Son chooses to reveal him." (10:21–22)

In the Spirit, the Son's joy wells up in grateful thanks to the Father for the life, knowledge, trust, and love they share. This is the Son's identity: to be given life and all things by the Father in the Spirit. God the Father's very identity is to be the one who begets and loves the Son in the unity of the Holy Spirit. That is who the Father is. He was never without his Son to love, and the Son was never without his Father to love. This means that God's being in eternal, self-sufficient aseity is no somber abstraction and no departure from the goodness of Jesus. It is the very fountainhead of his—and our—happiness. Jonathan Edwards wrote, "God undoubtedly infinitely loves and delights in himself. . . . The infinite happiness of the Father consists in the enjoyment of his Son."[1]

---

1 Jonathan Edwards, "Discourse on the Trinity," in *The Works of Jonathan Edwards*, vol. 21, *Writings on the Trinity, Grace, and Faith*, ed. Sang Hyun Lee (New Haven, CT: Yale University Press, 2003), 117.

Indeed, "God's love is primarily to himself and his infinite delight is in himself, *in the Father and the Son loving and delighting in one another.*"[2] This satisfied, delighted fullness of being means there is no lack of love and happiness in God. The Father's default way of being is to be filled with pleasure in fellowship with his Son in the Spirit. This love is ground zero of all the blessings that spill out on us in the gospel.

"It Will Flame Out"

The very fact that God ever created the world is testament to the explosion of love from within the triune life. Richard Sibbes saw it like this:

> The Father, Son and Holy Ghost were happy in themselves and enjoyed one another before the world was. But that God delights to communicate and spread his goodness, there had never been a creation nor a redemption. God uses his creatures not for defect of power, that he can do nothing without them, *but for the spreading of his goodness.*[3]

From the fellowship of Father, Son, and Spirit, superabundant goodness *spreads*. God's life and love overflow in his creation of the world. Since he always had his Son at his side, it is in the Father's very nature to give to another.

Make no mistake, the creation was not necessary: it was totally gratuitous. God doesn't *need* there to be a creation, but all things exist *because of* his happy self-existence. Because of God's aseity, we can know that all his works are gracious.

2   Edwards, *Works*, 21:118 (emphasis added).
3   Richard Sibbes, "The Successful Seeker," in *The Works of Richard Sibbes*, ed. Alexander B. Grosart, vol. 6 (Edinburgh: Banner of Truth, 1983), 113 (emphasis added).

We associate God's grace most readily with the forgiveness of sins, but long before there was any sin, God brought creation into being out of unbounded love. He gives life and being freely, for "his very life, being and goodness is yeasty: spreading out that there might be more that is truly good."[4] That God can create something and call that creation—something other than himself!—"good" is a mark of his ebullient fullness. Paul's address to the Athenians, mentioned above, continues this way: "He himself gives to all mankind life and breath and everything" (Acts 17:25). Job recognizes the same:

> In his hand is the life of every living thing
> and the breath of all mankind. (12:10)

Filled up by the Lord, creation—just by existing—is a living testament to his kindness. Sibbes said that God "delights to spread his beams and his influence in inferior things, to make all things fruitful. Such a goodness is in God as is in a fountain, or in the breast that loves to ease itself of milk."[5]

That is why creation is as it is. God's works speak of his glorious goodness. His work of creation, after all, began with a blaze of light (Gen. 1:3). He places lights in the firmament that repeatedly draw our eyes and hearts to remembrance of him in his own radiance, as Psalm 19:1 testifies,

> The heavens declare the glory of God,
> and the sky above proclaims his handiwork.

And Isaiah writes:

---

4   Michael Reeves, *Delighting in the Trinity: An Introduction to the Christian Faith* (Downers Grove, IL: IVP Academic, 2012), 47.
5   Sibbes, *Works*, 6:113.

Lift up your eyes on high and see:
　　who created these?
He who brings out their host by number,
　　calling them all by name;
by the greatness of his might
　　and because he is strong in power,
　　not one is missing. (40:26)

From those stars to the sand on the seashore, and from polar ice caps to equatorial palm trees, the world is shot through with the liberal and lively love of the Lord. Gerard Manley Hopkins's poem captures something of creation's borrowed glory.

The world is charged with the grandeur of God.
　　It will flame out, like shining from shook foil;
　　It gathers to a greatness, like the ooze of oil
Crushed. Why do men then now not reck his rod?
Generations have trod, have trod, have trod;
　　And all is seared with trade; bleared, smeared with toil;
　　And wears man's smudge and shares man's smell: the soil
Is bare now, nor can foot feel, being shod.

And for all this, nature is never spent;
　　There lives the dearest freshness deep down things;
And though the last lights off the black West went
　　Oh, morning, at the brown brink eastward, springs—
Because the Holy Ghost over the bent
　　World broods with warm breast and with ah! bright wings.[6]

---

6 Gerard Manley Hopkins, "God's Grandeur," in *Poems and Prose* (London: Penguin Classics, 1985), 27.

The creation is an expression of God's desire for us to know and enjoy him, just as Father, Son, and Spirit have known and enjoyed one another in perfect eternal fellowship. The Heidelberg Catechism asks what we mean in confessing our belief in "God, the Father almighty, creator of heaven and earth," and answers this way:

> That the eternal Father of our Lord Jesus Christ,
> who out of nothing created heaven and earth
> and everything in them,
> who still upholds and rules them
> by his eternal counsel and providence,
> is my God and Father
> because of Christ the Son.
>
> I trust God so much that I do not doubt
> he will provide
> whatever I need
> for body and soul,
> and will turn to my good
> whatever adversity he sends upon me
> in this sad world.
>
> God is able to do this because he is almighty God
> and desires to do this because he is a faithful Father.[7]

What a comfort it is to have an eternally full and self-existent God. It means he is for us an anchor of unchanging faithfulness (James 1:17), perfectly free to do just as he chooses (Ps. 115:3), and unassailable by any evil or wickedness that would try to stand in his way

---

7 Heidelberg Catechism, Christian Reformed Church (website), https://www.crcna.org/, PDF, answer 26.

(Job 42:2). Beyond this alone, though, what a joy to have a God whose glory is to share himself rather than hide himself. He presents himself to be known, his fatherly goodness to be enjoyed, and his life to be received. And his aseity, simplicity, and immutability mean that these wonders never cease. John Howe, the Puritan preacher and chaplain to Oliver Cromwell, wrote that when delighting yourself in this God, "you will still find a continual spring, unexhausted fullness, a fountain never to be drawn dry."[8]

Say No to Needy Gods

The glorious fullness of the living God revealed in Jesus sets him apart from all other gods. His innermost being is a sun of light, life, and warmth, always shining out: radiant and outgoing. Other gods, however, are always pits of grasping neediness.

Throughout the Old Testament, the idols that tempt the Israelites are constantly characterized as הֶבֶל (hevel), "emptiness." In Ecclesiastes, the word is translated "vanity": "I have seen everything that is done under the sun, and behold, all is vanity and a striving after wind" (1:14). This emptiness is insubstantial nothingness, the flimsy consolations of Job's friends (Job 21:34), and the fast-evaporating thoughts of human beings (Ps. 94:11). It is the exact opposite of כָּבוֹד (kavod), which speaks of substance and weight. When the Israelites turn to the gods of the nations around them, the Lord says,

> They have made me jealous with what is no god;
>   they have provoked me to anger with their idols
>   ["emptiness"]. (Deut. 32:21)

8   John Howe, *A Treatise of Delighting in God* (London: Seeley, 1825), 209.

In 2 Kings 17:15, the people of Israel "went after their false [or empty] idols [הֶבֶל] and became false [or empty, הָבַל]" themselves. These idols are empty and will hollow out those who worship them. They require the shedding of human blood (1 Kings 18:28) and the sacrifice of precious children (2 Kings 23:10); they cannot bring the rain (Jer. 14:22); and while they gladly take offerings, they cannot save in the times of trouble (Jer. 11:12).

With their horrifying cults and deceitful promises, the demonic gods of the nations around Israel are frequently called abominations, as in "Milcom the *abomination* of the Ammonites" (1 Kings 11:5) or "Chemosh the *abomination* of Moab" (2 Kings 23:13). This "abomination" is שִׁקּוּץ (*shiqquts*), a word that has to do with filth, soiled clothes (Nah. 3:6), and contamination. It would not be a word to say over a polite dinner. These idols were a pollution to the people of God (Jer. 7:30) and had to be "removed" (Jer. 4:1) and "cast away" (Ezek. 20:7), worth only ejecting as useless, disgusting waste. Jews would refer to Satan as *Beelzebul* ("Lord of the Flies," cf. 2 Kings 1:6) since, as the prince of demons (Matt. 12:24), his stench would surely attract the largest swarms of flies. All gods that would set themselves against the true and living God are just such an offense to believers; so worthless are they that, good for nothing else, they are to be flushed away and forgotten.

The futility of false gods is even conceded by their worshipers. In Acts 19, when Paul has preached the gospel in Ephesus, Demetrius the idol maker complains, "There is danger not only that this trade of ours may come into disrepute but also that the temple of the great goddess Artemis may be counted as nothing, and that she may even be deposed from her magnificence, she whom all Asia and the world worship" (vv. 27–28). This is quite an admission! Artemis is "nothing" without her temple and her worshipers, who could leave her at any moment. In the riot that follows, the crowds chant, "Great is Artemis of the Ephesians!" for two solid hours (Acts 19:34), but the truth is that she entirely *relies* on these her followers.

It is not only pagan gods that have this problem. When the philosopher Aristotle considered God's goodness, he realized that it meant God being good *to* something or someone. Picturing God as "the uncaused cause," he argued that God was surely *eternally* good to his creation—that which he caused. Aristotle's logical conclusion was that creation must itself be eternal. Even more significantly, his argument meant that his god *needed* the world. He simply would not be good—in other words, he would not be himself—without it. Monadic, single-person gods will always have this problem. Only the triune God can be truly self-existent *and* all good.

All false gods *need* worship and service and sustenance. Not being self-existent or full in themselves, they demand, consume, and are never satisfied. Like hungry and irritable toddlers, they tend to throw tantrums and strike fear into their devotees. They are never satisfied and must always be on the take. Meanwhile, nothing about our God is withdrawn or protective, as though he were lacking or needy. He alone is eternally good, loving, and full of life. It is his very nature to abound, to give, and to radiate. His generosity replenishes the lives of his creatures each day as we wake and take our first breaths.

You Open Your Hand

God's fullness sets him apart not only from idols but also from us creatures. Within two verses of the creation of Adam and Eve, we are told that they will need to eat to stay alive, and so the Lord provides them with food (Gen. 1:29). Humanity is, by nature, dependent and needy. Not only do we receive our life in the first place (unlike the Lord), but also we need to eat, drink, and sleep in order for that life to continue. God, who has life in himself, must *bestow* it on us, and God, who is eternal, must *preserve* us in that life. Like the rest of the creation, we rely on the provision of the Lord for all the things we need.

> The eyes of all look to you,
>> and you give them food in due season.
> You open your hand;
>> you satisfy the desire of every living thing. (Ps. 145:15–16)

Every time we hungrily sit down to a meal or collapse into bed, we are confronted with our own limits and finitude—our need to take something in before we can begin to give out again. It is no accident that we are this way. Sometimes we feel weary and worn out because of our sinfulness and the trials of this fallen world, but the fact of our total reliance on God is built in to our original design. In Genesis 2:7, we read that the Lord made Adam from the dust of the ground, forming his physical body from the earth, so that for a moment he was nothing more than a lump of clay. Even his name is a play on the Hebrew word for "earth" or "ground." But God "breathed into his nostrils the breath of life," and it is this kiss of life that transformed the mud man into a "living creature."

This "being" of ours—often translated elsewhere as "soul," the very principle of our life—is intimately connected to another concept in Hebrew: the *throat* (the exact same word is translated this way in Isa. 5:14 and Ps. 107:9, for example). The human soul is like an open throat. For you to be a "living being" is to be like a newly hatched chick in the nest. Not yet able to fly or hunt for yourself, you open your beak wide and cry out for the provision of your parents. You are created to desire and crave—and to have poured into you from outside—life and sustenance, whether physical or spiritual. For this reason, the very soul of a person can "thirst for God" like a deer panting for water (Ps. 42:2) or a man in a "dry and weary land where there is no water" (Ps. 63:1). To be human is to be a thirsting and hungry throat: to rely on, receive from, and eat and drink from the living God.

The Lord has made us this way to show that he alone is the source of life and that we must go to him for it. Every harvest time, it is our God who "crowns the year with his bounty" and whose "wagon tracks overflow with abundance" (Ps. 65:11). He is the one who has "filled the hungry with good things" (Luke 1:53). He is the one who "did good by giving you rains from heaven and fruitful seasons, satisfying your hearts with food and gladness" (Acts 14:17). Our very nature as human beings is to be contingent, always looking to God for life and everything. Maximus the Confessor, writing in the seventh century, saw that it was God's own delight to satisfy us in this way. "God who is beyond fullness did not bring creatures into being out of any need of his, but that he might enjoy their proportionate participation in him and that he might delight in his works seeing them delighted and ever insatiably satisfied with the one who is inexhaustible."[9]

Full and Empty Living

There is no feeling quite so alarming as that moment when, late at night and on unfamiliar roads, you realize your car is almost out of fuel. Will there be somewhere to fill up nearby? Will the place be open? Your eyes are fixed on the fuel gauge. With heart thumping and palms sweating as the miles go by, you envision your car sucking

---

9   Maximus the Confessor, *The Four Hundred Chapters on Love*, trans. George C. Berthold (Mahwah, NJ: Paulist, 1985), 67.

up the last drops and fumes from the tank before spluttering and juddering, leaving you stranded.

For too many of us, our experience of the Christian life and of mission feels similarly precarious. Our view of God has slowly become distorted and skewed, so we do not set out filled with joy and satisfaction in him. In our efforts to serve the demanding god of our imaginations, our discipleship and evangelism feel eked out, because they are not fueled by an all-generous, giving God. We run on the fumes of our own devotion and spiritual energy.

If our God is not full, neither will we be.

Devoted dog owners are said to take on the likeness of their pets, and children adopt the fashion choices of their sporting or musical heroes, but we are even more profoundly shaped by our God or gods. False gods need not be handcrafted statues for them to steal life from us. When we set our hearts and hopes on anything that is not the living God, we are thrown back on ourselves. Gods that cannot speak will need us to find words. Gods that cannot carry us will need us to pick ourselves up. Gods that cannot freely love will need us to make ourselves loveable. Whether our god is reputation, possessions, or relationships, we will be let down. Exhausting our own supplies, and with no supernatural help from such non-Gods as these, we will become as demanding and oppressive as they appear to us.

Of course the same goes for our view of the Lord. We can, by our sin and ignorance, find ourselves worshiping an idol and believing it to be him. Like the Israelites at Mount Sinai, we gather around a golden calf, telling ourselves it was *that* god that brought us out of slavery and honoring it as though it were the Lord (Ex. 32:4–5). When we ascribe to the Lord any neediness, emptiness, or self-aggrandizement, our "theology of glory" has been allowed to trample over the "theology of the cross"; we have inserted our own ideas about him and neglected how he has shown himself to us. The golden calf has usurped the Passover Lamb. Christians in name only, we will not enjoy or love God but feel he is distant and silent. And, believing that our illusion is the true and living God above all others, how could we not despair? Without Jesus showing us the truth, a God with ultimate power and aseity could only ever cast a long and menacing shadow over us and drive us to misery.

When we come to look at God in the light of Christ, we are set free from all such idols and distortions. This God is, by nature, an eternal spring of happiness and goodness, completely and irrepressibly *full*—full of glory, full of life, and full of blessing for the world. He is no black hole, eternally swallowing up glory, but an everlasting sun, *radiating* glory to the farthest reaches of our darkness. In Christ, God beams upon us, reveals his goodness, and shares himself with us. When we consider the inner life of God, revealed in Christ and his cross, we meet a superabundant, generous Father in heaven who does not cease to pour out blessing on the world and on his creatures.

In this way, the God whose very life is marked by the delighted mutual enjoyment of Father, Son, and Spirit is the foundation for our own happiness. We were created to satisfy ourselves in the love of God, and we are most full of joy when we drink at the overflowing fountain of his life, rather than sucking on the feeble fumes of our own. His happy fullness—and our derived enjoyment of him—is the heartbeat of mission, too. It is God's own delighted, overflowing fullness that defines mission in the first place, for before it was ever a task given to the church, it was the disposition of God to communicate, give, and fill up. It is our knowledge of God and our enjoyment of him that fills *us* up and sends *us* out with his own life, love, and happiness into the world to communicate and bless as he does.

4

Emptiness

IF GOD IS REALLY SO GOOD, surely mission must be the easiest work in the world. Simply hold out Jesus in his gospel, and people should come flocking.

Of course, that's not how it is. Quite the opposite. Bizarrely, wonderful good news of free grace is a tough sell. People dislike not just the idea of God in general but the message of the gospel specifically. Late in his life, George Orwell recalled that as a schoolboy, he hated Jesus and even felt sympathy toward Judas and Pontius Pilate, who had betrayed and executed him.[1] Orwell's attitude may well have been the perversity of a schoolboy, but it expresses something of our natural hostility toward God and the gospel.

Human beings are fallen, and this is why we do not intuitively worship, trust, and love God. The radiance of God's glory shines not into neutrality but into *darkness*. Indeed, Paul writes that our hearts are "darkened" (Rom. 1:21) because we reject the Lord. The truth is that human beings, originally made in the image of God to love

---

1 George Orwell, *The Complete Works of George Orwell: It Is What I Think* (London: Secker & Warburg, 1986), 379.

and enjoy him, reflecting his radiance in the world, have become *in*glorious through turning away from him.

Made for Glory

We were created to live in the presence and blessing of God. The first couple, Adam and Eve, were placed in the paradise of Eden, which God himself had planted for them, and where they were to enjoy fellowship with him (Gen. 2:8; 3:8). Bursting with beauty and gracious provision (Gen. 2:9), Eden was to be the base from which humanity could "be fruitful and multiply" across the face of the earth (Gen. 1:28), filling it with life. Adam and Eve were to rule over the creation, stewarding and caring for the world on behalf of the Lord (Gen. 1:28). In his "image and likeness" (Gen. 1:26), they were to be agents of his spreading goodness.

Paul writes that Adam was a "type," or pattern, of Christ, "the one who was to come" (Rom. 5:14), because his purpose was to picture the one man who has always enjoyed the love of his Father (John 17:24), to whom every knee would one day bow (Phil. 2:10), and who would come to fill all things (Eph. 1:23). Adam is even called "the son of God" in Luke 3:38, so much was he meant to be *like* the eternal Son of the Father. This was God's design for humanity: that we would delight ourselves in the love of God, image him in the creation, and reach to the ends of the earth in abundant fruitfulness. Here is the root of our sense of dignity, the reason we feel an itch for purpose and significance. We were created *for* glory and to *be* glorious, like our God.

Enslaved to Emptiness

Sin unraveled all this. More than simply disobeying a command and getting himself into trouble, Adam in his fall turned away from the Lord, the fountain of all life and love. The aftermath was devastating, for in denying God, Adam also defaced himself, enslaving himself and all his children to emptiness.

The temptation that arose at the tree was to look for satisfaction in something other than the Lord. The fruit itself was "good for food," "a delight to the eyes," and desirable "to make one wise" (Gen. 3:6), but the serpent assured Eve, "Your eyes will be opened, and *you will be like God*, knowing good and evil" (Gen. 3:5). The tantalizing promise of the serpent was greater glory for humanity *away* from God. In that moment, Paul writes, Adam and Eve "exchanged the truth about God for a lie and worshiped and served the creature rather than the Creator, who is blessed forever" (Rom. 1:25). Their delight, desire, and worship were all transferred in a moment away from the Lord and onto a created thing. It was, in one sense, the fruit; in another deeper sense, it was themselves. The fall was a selfish rearrangement of the order of everything, beginning with God. It was a fall into idolatry. Rather than living outward in loving obedience to the Lord and therefore in a posture of blessing toward the creation, humanity rejected fellowship with God and took from and relied upon the creation. The fall was a kind of implosion as Adam and Eve withdrew *inward* in sinister self-interest.

Having turned away from the God of glorious fullness, they condemned themselves to chase the fullness they now lacked in created things that could never meet their needs and desires. Instead of savoring God's lavish supply of food in Eden, they found themselves in a battle to survive on the earth over which they were meant to rule (Gen. 3:17–19). Instead of the joyful multiplying of human life, procreation was now to be marked by pain and discord (Gen. 3:16). Instead of enjoying endless life in communion with God, they were now to die, returning to the ground as the dust from which Adam was taken (Gen. 3:19). Eve thought that eating the fruit would make her "like God"—something *more* than she already was. Yet, in the eating, she and her husband became far *less* than they were. They had, of course, been created to be like God in the first place, but now, heeding the whisper of the serpent, they were quite *unlike* God. Their fellowship with him was cut off, and the pair were banished from Eden (Gen. 3:22–24). How the mighty had fallen! This was a fall not only from moral innocence and purity but from fullness and glory.

"Man is like a breath [הֶבֶל, *hevel*]," says David; "his days are like a passing shadow" (Ps. 144:4). "What wrong did your fathers find in me" the Lord asks in Jeremiah 2:5,

> that they went far from me
> and went after worthlessness [הֶבֶל, *hevel*] and became worthless?

It is now impossible for us to imagine life and humanity before the fall of Adam. We will generally tend to underestimate the ruinous consequences of the fall on ourselves and the world because we have not even a moment's experience of life untouched by it. Even as we recognize beauty in broken humanity, the capacity for great achievements or moments of compassion and altruism, we only see a faint glimmer of the glory for which we were meant. We were supposed to be like Jesus Christ, the radiance of God's glory, living *from* and *to* him, shining his light into the world. But in our turning away from our God, the glory has departed: we are darkened, shriveled, and empty. Like a laptop computer with the power cord unplugged, even the life we appear to hold within us is gradually ebbing away. Disconnected from the ever-full source of life and light and love, we are but waning shadows of all we were intended to be.

> All flesh is grass,
> and all its beauty is like the flower of the field.

The grass withers, the flower fades
> when the breath of the LORD blows on it;
> surely the people are grass.

The grass withers, the flower fades
> but the word of our God will stand forever. (Isa. 40:6–8)

Hollowed Out in the City of Man

Augustine wrote his *City of God* in the wake of Rome's catastrophic fall in AD 410. The ruin of the world's greatest capital was, for him, a parable of the fall: the disastrous attempt of humanity to build an "earthly city" on man-made foundations rather than to look for the heavenly City of God (Heb. 11:16; 12:22). The City of Man is the abode of Cain, who first took a human life (Gen. 4:8); it is Babel and Babylon (Gen. 11:4; Ps. 137:8); it is where the flesh wars against the Spirit (Gal. 5:17). With God's glory exchanged for the lie and living our own way in the desires of our flesh, we actually live out a devilish falsehood about what humanity ought to be.[2] The rotten fruit of this deathly life is shown in Galatians 5:19–21: "Now the works of the flesh are evident: sexual immorality, impurity, sensuality, idolatry, sorcery, enmity, strife, jealousy, fits of anger, rivalries, dissensions, divisions, envy, drunkenness, orgies, and things like these."

Though we are created to love God, our desires are turned to lusts. Though made to brim full of bestowed life, we take it from others (even when we do not physically kill as Cain did, Matt. 5:21–22). Though designed to enjoy God and others, we abuse and take advantage of them. Our sin *de*humanizes us and diminishes us. Like Adam and Eve, we quite easily believe that sin will be enjoyable or

---

2 Augustine, *City of God* 14.4.

will benefit us in some way: we are drawn to let our eyes linger on images they should pass over, to take what is not our own, and to look for ways to aggrandize ourselves. While all the craving, taking, and hoarding seem so alluring to us, we most often find that it leaves us feeling achingly hollow. Far from adding to us or building us up, sin makes us far *less* human than we are meant to be, slowly eating us. Indeed, Augustine said, "No sooner do we begin to live in this dying body, than we begin to move ceaselessly towards death."[3]

C. S. Lewis also sketched our emptiness in his novel *The Great Divorce*, in which he imagined a bus ride from hell to heaven. While Lewis was writing an allegory about those ultimate destinations, he used it to pick out a contrast between all spiritual emptiness and spiritual wholeness, sin and goodness, fallenness and redemption. Hellishness—aside from its eternal reality and magnitude—is expressed and anticipated in humanity's *present* fallenness. In the book, hell is a dingy and miserable "grey town," and those who inhabit it are ghostly shadows of real humanity, irritated by light and entirely caught up in themselves.

> I glanced round the bus. Though the windows were closed, and soon muffed, the bus was full of light. It was cruel light. I shrank from the faces and forms by which I was surrounded. They were all fixed faces, full not of possibilities but of impossibilities, some gaunt, some bloated, some glaring with idiotic ferocity, some drowned beyond recovery in dreams; but all, in one way or another, distorted and faded. One had a feeling that they might fall to pieces at any moment if the light grew much stronger.[4]

---

3 Augustine of Hippo, *The City of God*, in *St. Augustin's City of God and Christian Doctrine*, vol. 2 of *A Select Library of the Nicene and Post-Nicene Fathers of the Christian Church*, series 1, ed. Philip Schaff, trans. Marcus Dods (Buffalo, NY: Christian Literature, 1887), 249.

4 C. S. Lewis, *The Great Divorce* (London: Bles, 1946; repr., London: Collins, 2015), 17.

The wraiths on the bus to heaven were tired and worn, yet compulsively busy with self-justification. They were paranoid and on edge, incessantly bitter and negative, aggressive and selfish. So undone by sin, they were almost unreal, "man-shaped stains on the brightness of [the] air" in heaven, where "the grass did not bend under their feet: even the dew drops were not disturbed."[5] One ghost had once been a well-dressed woman, but her "shadows of finery looked ghastly in the morning light."[6] While heaven was painfully, excessively real for its pallid visitors, the grey town embodied the inner life of its inhabitants. Because they quarreled so much, they constantly moved to new houses in order to be alone, so the town was infinitely expanding in size and yet ever more empty. The tragedy of the story was the inability of the ghosts to appreciate and enjoy the beauty of heavenly reality and the bright "Solid People" they encounter on their visit, so deeply were they attached to their own grey way of being.

Since Adam drew away from fellowship with the God of fullness and life (John 1:4; 17:3), humanity has been gnawingly empty of that life. When we are left alone in our sin, our emptiness and lifelessness spread in and from us like a cancer. Paul writes that "sin came into the world through one man, and death through sin, and so *death spread to all men*" (Rom. 5:12). The continuation of this Adamic kind of life is nothing but death.

The Image Defaced

Our fallen emptiness means we cannot be radiant as we were meant to be. Humanity, made in the image of God, should shine on the earth with reflected light. We were created to have fulfilling fellowship

---

5   Lewis, *The Great Divorce*, 20–21.
6   Lewis, *The Great Divorce*, 59.

with God and so to glow with his beauty and happiness, like his Son, drawing all creation to enjoy our God. As Athanasius put it in the mid-fourth century, we were created to have our being "God-ward in a freedom unembarrassed by shame" just as does God the Word in whose image we were formed.[7] When, in the fall, Adam ceased to contemplate or look to God and looked instead to himself (even to his own body in its nakedness and vulnerability, Gen. 3:7), the crucial bond between the divine image and the image bearer was broken. The image of God in humanity was defaced, and the glory dimmed. Having no glory of our own, we have nothing to give out. Athanasius said that, "because death and corruption were gaining ever firmer hold on them, the human race was in process of destruction. Man, who was created in God's image and in his possession of reason reflected the very Word Himself, was disappearing, and the work of God was being undone."[8]

Adam's loss of glory became the family trait. As well as being infected with his guilt and his death, each of us bears his likeness in behavior, "for all have sinned and fall short of the glory of God" (Rom. 3:23). It would be wrong to say that fallen people no longer bear the image of God at all: sin has not entirely destroyed all that God created. Nevertheless, the image is spoiled and marred such that we do not shine out with the glory of God. Instead, as Scripture presses home again and again, we languish in darkness and are blind to his light. Darkness is where the wicked are cut off (1 Sam. 2:9); it is the doom of the stumbling wicked (Prov. 4:19) and the prevail-

---

7   Athanasius of Alexandria, *Against the Heathen*, in *St. Athanasius: Select Works and Letters*, vol. 4 of *A Select Library of the Nicene and Post-Nicene Fathers of the Christian Church*, series 2, ed. Philip Schaff and Henry Wace, trans. Archibald T. Robertson (New York: Christian Literature, 1892), 4–5.

8   Athanasius of Alexandria, *On the Incarnation* (New York: SVS, 1996), 39.

ing spiritual atmosphere of the fallen world (Eph. 6:12). Darkness frequently speaks of the judgment of God: darkness fell over Egypt in the final plague before the Passover (Ex. 10:21–23), and fallen angels sit in "chains of gloomy darkness to be kept until the judgment" (2 Pet. 2:4). The Lord of light himself is even said to dwell in "thick darkness" at times (Ex. 20:21; 1 Kings 8:12; Ps. 97:2), in one sense mercifully masking his dazzling brightness while also dramatically demonstrating the contrast between his glorious goodness and our evil. Perhaps the most dramatic darkness that expresses human fallenness is the darkness that descended at the crucifixion of Jesus. From midday until three in the afternoon, darkness covered the land as the Lord died under the judgment of God for our sin (Mark 15:33–34). As George Matheson wrote, at the cross "I lay in dust, life's glory dead,"[9] for what Christ bore in himself was precisely what Adam had brought on humanity in the fall.

Even in our darkness, we do not naturally look for God or seek the restoration of his image in us. In fact, we content ourselves with the situation we are in, like the "dog that returns to his vomit" (Prov. 26:11). Fallen humanity is bound and captive to sin (Rom. 7:24) and hostile to God (Rom. 8:7). We are resistant and defensive, even when the gospel is proclaimed to us. It is a reflex action of sinners to mock the evangelist, refuse to cross the threshold of a church, or close down any conversation that might lead toward Jesus Christ. Athanasius compares this natural human situation to a man plunged into the inky blackness of the sea and unable to see the light. With water above and below, and with his eyes turned down, he quickly comes to imagine that the darkness surrounding him is all there is.

9 George Matheson, "O Love That Wilt Not Let Me Go" (1882), https://hymnary.org.

With hardly a thought, he forgets the "knowledge and glory of God" and sets his sights on created things, "deifying" or worshiping them, rather than the Creator.[10]

What we look at and settle our hearts on will always shape us and emboss itself on our souls. With our eyes off God in his glory, and forever flitting about in the darkest corners, we are gradually formed into the image of creatures that deprive us of the life we miss and cannot satisfy us or restore us to our proper place. As Luther had it in his exposition of the first commandment, instead of worshiping God who is the source of all good and help and consolation, our hearts "stand gaping at something else," which cannot help us.[11] Anyone who has struggled with an addiction or a besetting sin will know the strangely enthralling power of the very thing we know to hurt and reduce us. However frustrated and unfulfilled we find ourselves, we nevertheless settle into unhappy cycles of worshiping nothingness, with nothing to gain and nothing to give out.

Perhaps the most perplexing response we encounter in evangelism is not so much anger but apathy. This reaction may frustrate the evangelist, but it should provoke our compassion. It is the fruit of a heart that is simultaneously deeply unsatisfied and without hope of satisfaction. The emptiness of sin is so profound that it leaves us hardened and stagnant.

Man "Curved in upon Himself"

This craving emptiness leaves us strangely wrapped up in ourselves. Without a sight of God's glory and unable to reflect his image to

10 Athanasius, *Against the Heathen*, 8.

11 Martin Luther, "The Large Catechism," in *Concordia: The Lutheran Confessions: A Reader's Edition of the Book of Concord*, ed. Paul Timothy McCain (St. Louis, MO: Concordia, 2006), 360.

the world, we become insular and caved in. We were created to desire and enjoy God, finding a fulfillment in him that allows us to be happy and fruitful, as he is. Now that we are enslaved to selfishness and idolatry, untamed desires fiercely rule over us: we are more hungry than we are satisfied, more needy than we are generous. Paul writes of sinful humanity, "Their end is destruction, their god is their belly, and they glory in their shame, with minds set on earthly things" (Phil. 3:19).

When Augustine described the City of God and the City of Man, he wrote that while the first was built on the love of God, the second was founded on the love of self:

> Accordingly, two cities have been formed by two loves: the earthly by the love of self, even to the contempt of God; the heavenly by the love of God, even to the contempt of self. The former, in a word, glories in itself, the latter in the Lord. For the one seeks glory from men; but the greatest glory of the other is God, the witness of conscience. The one lifts up its head in its own glory; the other says to its God, "Thou art my glory, and the lifter up of mine head."[12]

It is vintage Augustine to see here two powerful *loves* going to war. He sees that our effort to lift up our own heads yields a bent-over, deforming incurvature of ourselves. To turn our love inward and imagine we will find life and goodness there is not strong and healthy but ugly and damaging. Lewis drives home the sheer unattractiveness of this self-love in *The Great Divorce*. "Friend," says one the heavenly citizens to a ghost, "could you only for a moment, fix your mind on something not yourself?"[13] No doubt it is a question we have

---

12 Augustine, *The City of God*, 282–83.
13 Lewis, *The Great Divorce*, 62.

silently asked at times, of others and of ourselves. When another of the ghosts meets a resident of heaven—an old acquaintance whom he knows to have been a murderer—he is furious at their divergent destinies. "'Look at me now,' said the Ghost, slapping its chest (but the slap made no noise). 'I gone straight all my life. I don't say I was a religious man and I don't say I had no faults, far from it. But I done my best all my life, see? I done my best by everyone, that's the sort of chap I was.'"[14]

He insists that he "has his rights" as a result of this upstanding life, and when his companion explains that it would be far better *not* to have his rights, the conversation reveals his self-justifying hardness of heart:

> "That's just what I say. I haven't got my right. I always done my best and I never done anything wrong. And what I don't see is why I should be put below a bloody murderer like you."
>
> "Who knows whether you will be? Only be happy and come with me."
>
> "What do you keep arguing on for? I'm only telling you the sort of chap I am. I only want my rights, I'm not asking for anybody's bleeding charity."
>
> "Then do. At once. Ask for the Bleeding Charity. Everything is here for the asking and nothing can be bought."[15]

Martin Luther saw that even sincere-looking Christian devotion can be a means of preoccupation with the self. "Scripture describes man as so curved in upon himself that he uses not only physical but even spiritual goods for his own purposes and in all things seeks only

---

14 Lewis, *The Great Divorce*, 27.
15 Lewis, *The Great Divorce*, 28.

himself."[16] Living this way, Pharisees can look down their noses at tax collectors (Luke 18:9–14), and older brothers can crackle with jealousy at younger brothers (Luke 15:11–32), rightly identifying flagrant sin in others and yet nurturing it like a pet in their own hearts.

Paul relates in Romans 7:15–25 his experience of confused introspection at his destructive actions: "For I do not do the good I want, but the evil I do not want is what I keep on doing" (v. 19). It is a familiar picture to us all. We give ourselves to behavior we hate, and even in indulging ourselves, we resent ourselves all the more. As much as we are slavishly following what Thomas Cranmer called the "devices and desires of our own hearts," we feel somehow estranged from ourselves.

Mirror, Mirror, on the Wall . . .

Given all we have seen, it is no wonder that our culture is overrun with issues surrounding identity. Since the garden, we do not participate in the fullness of God's life, his image in us has been vandalized, and we are consumed with self-love. Sinners do not know who, why, or what they are. Many people want to improve themselves but simply do not know what "mended" or whole people would look like. Sensing our brokenness, we make wild stabs at solutions: political activism, radical moral codes, mindfulness, self-improvement, dieting fads, and so on.

Increasingly, self-assertion is seen as the key to real happiness, and so, in the brave quest for "authenticity," almost anything is to be applauded and honored. We recognize that some do not consider themselves beautiful, some are compelled to lie in their job applications,

---

16 Martin Luther, *Luther's Works*, vol. 25, *Lectures on Romans*, ed. Jaroslav Jan Pelikan, Hilton C. Oswald, and Helmut T. Lehmann (Philadelphia: Fortress; St. Louis, MO: Concordia, 1972), 345.

and others feel ill at ease with their biological sex. The answer to all this, we are led to believe, is to look in the mirror and to reach deep within to retrieve our "true self," increasingly accept it, and let it shine. However quirky, socially unacceptable, or controversial our actions, we are encouraged to be "true to ourselves," and those who do so most tenaciously are lionized. "You do you," says the world. This self-assertion is a kind of mission, but one driven by the empty self and not by the glorious God of heaven. It reaches out into the world not to give but to take.

Ours is a society utterly persuaded by this lie and largely unable to see the truth: all the talk of looking within and finding "it" within yourself will never solve the problem, because that *is* the problem. We are simply not designed for incurvature.

Not only within the church do people see the downsides of the great god of self. Psychologists and journalists are sounding the alarm about the dangers of social media, fearing that hours spent alone scrolling Instagram and TikTok for leisure are leading many into ill mental health.[17] While the endorphin rush of a message notification feels pleasurable (and can be addictive), someone else's holiday snaps can lead to a bout of "fear of missing out" and totally deflate us. Feeling our emptiness, we crave the praise and attention of other people, making ourselves hostage to their opinions. We may find ourselves emotionally leaning on others too heavily, forcing friendships or romantic relationships to carry a weight of expectation they are unable to bear. Anxiety, stress, depression, and loneliness soon follow. A 2021 study by Harvard Graduate School of Education found that in the wake of the coronavirus pandemic, 36 percent of Americans reported feeling

---

17 Michelle O'Reilly et al., "Is Social Media Bad for Mental Health and Wellbeing? Exploring the Perspectives of Adolescents," *Clinical Child Psychology and Psychiatry* 23, no. 4 (2018): 601–13.

lonely "frequently" or "almost all of the time." While loneliness has often been most associated with old age, this study found that 61 percent of young adults (ages eighteen to twenty-five) reported "serious loneliness."[18] For all the talk of learning to love ourselves, we ourselves are often the ones with whom we're most terrified of being left alone.

On the other hand, all the self-assertion leads to inevitable conflict between people. Not everybody will be comfortable with everyone else expressing himself or herself authentically; *your* "true self" may not entirely lend itself to the actualization of my own "true self." This may be expressed in naked bigotry ("I don't want to be around *your* kind of people!") or more subtly in pitting various groups of us against others, competing to be seen as most deserving of care or resources or representation. Minorities are set up against majorities, the young against the old, the poor against the rich, and there seems to be no end in sight to the war over who should be most free to do what they wish without the interference of anyone else. An atheist author like Douglas Murray can identify many of the features of this fallout: he suggests that the secular West has kept hold of the Christian concepts of guilt and shame but has no way to face them, instead boiling over into aggression. Murray is able even to prescribe "forgiveness" as a possible cure for our "madness," yet he does not offer any way to give or get it.[19]

How can people so well-fed on a diet of selfishness ever learn to behave in another way? The curses listed at the end of Deuteronomy 28

18 Richard Weissbourd, Milena Batanova, Virginia Lovison, and Eric Torres, "Loneliness in America: How the Pandemic Has Deepened an Epidemic of Loneliness and What We Can Do about It" (PDF), Harvard Graduate School of Education Making Caring Common Project, February 2021, 3, https://mcc.gse.harvard.edu/reports.

19 Douglas Murray, *The Madness of Crowds: Gender, Race and Identity* (London: Bloomsbury, 2019), 182.

for a people who have walked away from the Lord seem to ring true for our culture today:

> And among these nations you shall find no respite, and there shall be no resting place for the sole of your foot, but the LORD will give you there a trembling heart and failing eyes and a languishing soul. Your life shall hang in doubt before you. Night and day you shall be in dread and have no assurance of your life. In the morning you shall say, "If only it were evening!" and at evening you shall say, "If only it were morning!" because of the dread that your heart shall feel, and the sights that your eyes shall see. (vv. 65–67)

Such is the predicament of fallen humanity. Even Christians, redeemed and made righteous, will recognize something of themselves in this portrait of emptiness. For some it will resonate strongly with present struggles and experiences; for others, it will have brought back memories of what may seem like another life. However long ago we came to know Christ, and however much transformation we have known by his grace, there is in us still the "flesh" (Gal. 5:16), the "old self" (Rom. 6:6). While believers are no longer defined by their sin, it is a constant reminder of the reality of the world after Adam.

The emptiness and darkness of this present age form the context and backdrop of the mission of the church (Titus 2:12). They mark the condition of the people around us who must hear the gospel of the glory of God if they are to be set free. The church alone can see through the prevailing wisdom that hope lies within. The church alone can see that the city built on love of self is the city divided against itself that cannot stand (Matt. 12:25). The church alone can show the world where real fullness, happiness, and life are to be found.

5

Born in Zion

WHAT WAS GOD TO DO WITH HUMANITY, lost in this darkness and futility? God *reached out*. Christ came to *remake* us after his image.

This is where our mission began. For this renewal of human beings is not only the birth of *Christians* but the birth of *missionaries*, as we who once were darkness become "light in the Lord" (Eph. 5:8). We who once walked in all kinds of sin and worldliness, deserving the wrath of God, now find thankful hearts overflowing with the word of Christ and songs of praise (Col. 3:5–17).

When the psalmist applauds the glory of Zion in Psalm 87, he includes a surprising list of inhabitants: Rahab, Babylon, Philistia, Tyre, and Cush (v. 4). These are not Israelite cities and peoples: far from it, they are synonyms for the enemies of God, sinners, and strangers. Yet, the psalmist says of each, "This one was born there" in Zion (v. 4). The Lord himself registers the peoples and records the same verdict (v. 6). These Gentile outsiders are being counted as residents of Zion, included with Israel, fully belonging as though they were born in the city of God. By his grace, out of Rahab and Babylon, from darkness and nothingness, new life is found and a new identity is established. Those who once were far off, without hope and without God in the world, have been brought near and share in the calling of God's people to proclaim his gospel in the world with the apostles and prophets who have gone before (Eph. 2:11–13).

When the Most High establishes a new life in Christ, he transplants them from the old life of sin and emptiness to bear a brand-new identity in the image of God. He has always been on mission, as he eternally speaks his Word in the Spirit, but now *we*—freshly enlightened and enlivened—join with him in his gracious design to bless the world with his life.

The Image Restored

In Adam, humanity had slipped far from its noble purpose in creation, leaking life, falling short of God's glory, and turning in on itself in idolatry and selfishness. But Jesus Christ came into the world to turn us around. On the night the Savior was born, our dark world was flooded with light. The glory of the Lord shone around the shepherds as the angel announced his arrival, then "suddenly there was with the angel a multitude of the heavenly host" joyfully declaring, "Glory to God in the highest" (Luke 2:8–14). The brightness signaled that here was the Son, the radiance of the Father's glory, stepping into the spiritual darkness of the world.

Athanasius wrote that in the face of the evil dehumanizing of humanity, "the Word of God came in His own Person, because it was He alone, the Image of the Father Who could recreate man made after the Image."[1] This was the only way humanity could be saved: the true image taking our flesh to himself in order to renovate, remake, and restore it. This was to be a re-creation according to the original.

---

1   Athanasius of Alexandria, *On the Incarnation* (New York: SVS, 1996), 40–41.

This re-creation did not mean humanity going on the scrap heap and God starting again from scratch. Athanasius compared humanity to a beautiful portrait that had been stained and ruined. The artist, caring for his work, does not throw away the canvas and begin again with a new one, but lovingly restores his masterpiece. This was the work God had prized from the beginning: he would not willingly destroy it. Vitally, for this restoration to be done, the original subject must come and sit again to reestablish the likeness. So Christ "came and dwelt in our midst, in order that he might renew mankind made after Himself, and seek out His lost sheep" for, as Jesus himself said, he came "to seek and to save the lost" (Luke 19:10).[2] The tattered old canvas was about to be transformed.

Every moment of Jesus's life on earth was a display of humanity as it was always supposed to be. For the first time, a human being lived in the fullness of God's intentions for us. He perfectly loved, trusted, and obeyed his Father (John 14:31), and poured out his heart to him in prayer (Luke 6:12), even though he faced all the same temptation, weakness, and suffering we do (Heb. 2:18; 4:15). He was morally faultless himself but never lacked compassion for even the most notorious sinners (Mark 2:15–17). He exercised rule over the creation, stilling wind and waves (Matt. 8:27) and driving out the corruption of demons and diseases (Matt. 12:22–24). He amazed his disciples with words of truth that could only be God's own self-expression (Mark 10:24). He went silently to his death, giving himself in love for those who hated him (Mark 15:5). Full of life, gloriously good, and overflowing with kindness, Jesus was everything a human being is meant to be—the definitive likeness

2 Athanasius, *On the Incarnation*, 41–43.

of God, revealed in the original image himself. Here, at last, was a real man.

The Great Exchange

Our knee-jerk reaction to a portrait like that may be to pump ourselves up. Surely, here is the paragon of true human life to be emulated by the rest of us. It's true that the New Testament speaks of Christ setting us an example (Phil. 2:5–11; 1 Pet. 2:21) and of the Christian life as imitating him (1 Cor. 11:1; Eph. 5:1–2; 1 John 2:6), but it would be a mistake to think that the foundation of the renewed humanity is simply attempting to *copy* Jesus. That would very quickly turn us back in on ourselves in a kind of religious self-reliance, which would smell far more of Adam than of Christ. No, Jesus's renewal of humanity was not to be a matter of setting a better example than Adam did. Jesus did not come to give us the prototype of "your best life" to be replicated in ten easy steps. He came to redeem us.

Christ came to take hold of humanity, binding himself to us and us to himself. He came to take the old humanity to the cross with him and put it to death, raising us with him in his resurrection. "Father," he prayed shortly before his crucifixion, "I desire that they also, whom you have given me, *may be with me where I am*" (John 17:24). He became one of us so that we would become what he is, or as Irenaeus wrote, "The Word of God, our Lord Jesus Christ . . . did, through His transcendent love, become what we are, that He might bring us to be even what He is Himself."[3] In other words, salvation is an exchange. Christ came into the wreckage of humanity, taking

---

3 Irenaeus of Lyons, *Against Heresies*, in *The Apostolic Fathers with Justin Martyr and Irenaeus*, ed. Alexander Roberts, James Donaldson, and A. Cleveland Coxe, vol. 1 of *The Ante-Nicene Fathers* (Buffalo, NY: Christian Literature Company, 1885), 526.

all our sin and death to himself on the cross, and he raised us to the fellowship with the Father that he himself eternally had. This is not to say that we lose our humanity or metamorphize into deities, but that we receive a new kind of humanity—one defined no longer by Adam and his fall but by Christ, the image and Glory of God.

What Adam did to himself, he also did to all who were born from him, and so it is with Jesus and all who have life in him. While Adam sinned in Eden, selfishly taking what he wanted, Jesus sweated blood in Gethsemane as he prayed, "Nevertheless, not my will, but yours, be done" (Luke 22:42). While Adam bequeathed to us his condemnation, in Christ we inherit righteousness before God and an "abundance of grace" (Rom. 5:17). While Adam plunged humanity into sin, multiplying death from his body, Christ burst through death as the firstfruits and the head of a new humanity, full of life (1 Cor. 15:22; Col. 1:18). Now, his perfect life and righteousness are credited to us (2 Cor. 5:21), his resurrection is the guarantee of our own to come (Rom. 6:5), and we receive a whole catalog of spiritual blessings in and through him (Eph. 1:3–14). Christians really have Jesus for their own; they really have his Father as their Father, his Spirit as their Comforter. For this reason, Jesus can say in John 17:23 that the Father loves believers *even as he loves his Son*. Indeed, Jesus's prayer is "that *the love with which you have loved me* may be in them, and I in them" (John 17:26).

You Have Been Filled in Him

On the other side of the cross, this new human life, the restored artwork, is the "new self, which is being renewed in knowledge after the image of its creator" (Col. 3:10). It would be very easy to nod at this idea of renewal, thinking that our gratitude for Jesus's sacrifice and grace motivates us somehow to be better people. Yet the reality is something far deeper: in Jesus, we ourselves are actually changed.

We are reborn by the Holy Spirit and the word of God (John 3:6; 1 Pet. 1:23), nothing less than "a new creation" in him, with our old, sinful life behind us (2 Cor. 5:17). The same Spirit who filled, led, and empowered Jesus (Matt. 12:28; Luke 4:1) now dwells in us (Eph. 2:22). He is the "Spirit of Christ," who marks us out as belonging to Jesus and fills us with his life (Rom. 8:9–11). With our lives defined and shaped by Jesus Christ—knowing, enjoying, and worshiping him—we become like him by the Spirit's power. This life is ours immediately at conversion, when the old self dies with him (Rom. 6:5), but it also begins to suffuse and saturate our personalities, behaviors, and desires: the inward spiritual change begins to work its way out into our desires, thinking, speech, and relationships. We begin to take on the image of the one to whom we belong.

The Colossian church was spiritually vulnerable, facing pressure to turn aside from Jesus to various extraneous spiritual practices. Paul wrote to reassure them of the complete sufficiency of Jesus and the life they already had in him: "See to it that no one takes you captive by philosophy and empty deceit, according to human tradition, according to the elemental spirits of the world, and not according to Christ. *For in him the whole fullness of deity dwells bodily, and you have been filled in him*" (Col. 2:8–10). Here in Jesus Christ—and in him alone—is the fullness and life of God that we have lost and long for. With Jesus, we who naturally have nothing are given everything. Empty, hollow sinners are enriched, ennobled, and *filled* as we are united with the one who has in himself the fullness of God. From his fullness, we are given grace upon grace (John 1:16).

"Hearts Unfold like Flowers before Thee"

When we come to the cross of Christ and are filled by him, the first change we experience is in our relationship with God. The old idols that held us captive are swept away. The fears we had harbored about what God might be like evaporate. Our selfish focus on ourselves is shifted to the one who has become our delight. The Christian is a human being unraveled and released. We find ourselves increasingly warming with his love, unclenching our fists, and coming freely to adore and enjoy him. Unconsciously forgetting ourselves, we can sing,

Joyful, joyful, we adore Thee,
God of glory, Lord of love;
Hearts unfold like flowers before Thee,
opening to the sun above.[4]

Because we find this fullness and joy *outside* ourselves and in the Lord who gave himself for us, Peter writes that believers rejoice "with joy that is inexpressible and filled with *glory*" (1 Pet. 1:8). It is not a happiness that we need to gather and maintain within, like dwindling energy at the end of a long day. It is an extrinsic, external joy and satisfaction *in God*, whose fullness now fills us. Finding this unspeakable treasure outside ourselves, we become refreshingly un-self-obsessed. Once, we cringed and retreated before the light, but now we are blossoming flowers, soaking up the sunshine.

Many Christians take God seriously but also take themselves extremely seriously at the same time, often coming over as strict and spiky. The pride can be palpable and off-putting. Others take themselves very lightly and can look quite convincingly humble. But if everything in life is "just a bit of fun" and they avoid any depth or earnestness, then it is likely they also take God lightly. The Christian who has found satisfaction in Christ is able to take God with utmost

---

4 Henry Van Dyke, "Joyful, Joyful, We Adore Thee" (1907), https://hymnary.org.

seriousness and, at the same time, be quite relaxed about his or her reputation, image, and ambitions. This is the theology of the cross worked out in the believer's life. We know ourselves to be naturally empty and unimpressive, but happily place all our confidence and hope in Christ instead. People can think of us what they may, and our own hearts may sometimes whisper condemnation, but we are taken up with knowing and enjoying the Lord (1 John 3:20). As Richard Sibbes says:

> Often think with thyself, What am I? a poor sinful creature; but I have a righteousness in Christ that answers all. I am weak in myself, but Christ is strong, and I am strong in him. I am foolish in myself, but I am wise in him. What I want in myself I have in him. He is mine, and his righteousness is mine, which is the righteousness of God-man. Being clothed with this, I stand safe against conscience, hell, wrath, and whatsoever. Though I have daily experience of my sins, yet there is more righteousness in Christ, who is mine, and who is the chief of ten thousand, than there is sin in me. When thus we shall know Christ, then we shall know him to purpose.[5]

When Christ crucified is the center of your life and identity, people will read the liberation in your face. One of the "Bright People" in *The Great Divorce*, the man who had been a murderer, has a face that, says the narrator, "made me want to dance, it was so jocund, so established in its youthfulness."[6] This seems to aggravate a ghost, who asks if the former murderer is not ashamed of himself. He replies: "No. Not as

---

5   Richard Sibbes, *The Complete Works of Richard Sibbes*, ed. Alexander B. Grosart, vol. 2 (Edinburgh: Nichol, 1862), 147.
6   C. S. Lewis, *The Great Divorce* (London: Bles, 1946; repr., London: Collins, 2015), 26.

you mean. I do not look at myself. I have given up myself. I had to, you know, after the murder. That was what it did for me. And that was how everything began."[7]

True satisfaction and true humility always go together in this way. The humble Christian is a pleasure to be around and a pleasure to *be*. Whatever we may have done and whoever we may have been, the delight of absorbing ourselves in Christ rather than in ourselves is delicious freedom. Freed from the attempt to appease God and the charade of impressing others, we become both more honest and more openhearted. In humble, happy Christians, the glory of God is echoed back to him in gratitude. His glory was never simply blasted *at* us through loudspeakers but has been graciously revealed *for* us and shared with us. It cannot but be fruitful in us. There is a borrowed radiance and beauty in a person who knows what it means to be given something he or she could never earn or deserve. The overwhelmed gratitude of the son whose parents have bought him a car or paid the deposit on his house is a reflection back to them of their kindness. Thus, we glorify God as we reflect his beauty and mirror his light.

Gratified satisfaction always shows itself outwardly. After a wonderful, large meal, we will lean back in our chairs and groan happily. Satisfaction always issues in expression. So it is with our satisfaction in the fullness of God. Our enjoyment of his richness cannot and does not stay within. Once, we were turned inward to contemplate, love, and trust in ourselves. Now, turned inside out by the gospel of Jesus, not only do we look out from ourselves toward God in worship, but there is a second opening up we experience too. We radiate outward into the world.

---

7   Lewis, *The Great Divorce*, 27.

A Glorious Image

When empty ones are filled by the God of fullness, we become bright and glorious like him, for "we all, with unveiled face, beholding the glory of the Lord, are being transformed into the *same image* from *one degree of glory to another*" (2 Cor. 3:18). Glory is certainly a *future* hope for Christians (1 Pet. 5:10), and we know that on the last day a sight of the Lord will change us "in the twinkling of an eye" to be like him (1 Cor. 15:53; 1 John 3:2). Yet 2 Corinthians 3 speaks of our *present* transformation into Jesus's image, our becoming increasingly glorious, as we commune with him. Christians take on Jesus's radiance.

When Martin Luther first stumbled upon the gospel, reading Romans, he understood an astonishing aspect of the way God deals with believers. Luther was especially interested in the idea in Romans 1:17 that "the righteousness of God" is "revealed" in the gospel. He had always taken that to mean that, much like the law, the gospel declares God's complete holiness and purity over and against sinners. For this reason, even though he was a very dutiful monk, he could only ever hear the gospel as God condemning him, and so he found himself utterly devoid of assurance before God. His famous conversion turned on the realization that when the gospel revealed "the righteousness of God," it was as a *gift for sinners*, to be received with faith. God's righteousness is not something he keeps to himself to use as a shield; it is something of his own that he wishes to *share*. At this, Luther knew he was "born afresh."

What is worth noting here, though, is that in his giddy excitement, hardly daring to believe what he had seen, he ran through the Scriptures from memory and found "the whole face of scripture was changed." Why? He saw exactly the same dynamic at play in the work of God, which God works in us (Phil. 2:13); the strength of

God, by which he makes us strong (Col. 1:29); the wisdom of God, which makes us wise (James 3:13–17)—and also the glory of God.[8] The glory of God, that by which God makes *us glorious*—this is, of course, what Paul teaches in Romans 8:30, "Those whom he justified he also glorified," and 2 Thessalonians 2:14, "To this he called you through our gospel, so that you may obtain the glory of our Lord Jesus Christ." Life in Christ is the *glorification* of the believer. In fellowship with the one who is the Glory of God, how would we not be enlightened and enlivened?

Seeing and sharing in the glory of Jesus means that the fullness we have received spills over. When Moses returned from Mount Sinai, his face was beaming with light, "because he had been talking with God" (Ex. 34:29). So much so that when "Aaron and all the people of Israel saw Moses . . . the skin of his face shone, and they were afraid to come near him" (Ex. 34:30). Moses's time with the Lord caused him to shine with reflected light, and he had to wear a veil over his face until he next went in to speak with the Lord (Ex. 34:33–35). Paul writes in 2 Corinthians that we are like Moses in that we gaze upon the Lord, who is transforming us into his glorious image (3:18), but we are also *unlike* Moses in that we do not veil our faces but are "very bold" (3:12–13, 18). We are made to shine out the glory of God that we have seen in Christ, which God has shone into our hearts (4:6). This radiance is given so that it might shine out further. To put it another way, he who is the only spring of living water (Jer. 2:13) has caused that fountain to bubble up in us (John 4:14).

Here is the birth of our mission, for the Christian's new birth is a birth into a life in the image of the God who is always on mission.

---

8   Luther, "Autobiographical Fragment" (1545), in *Martin Luther*, ed. E. Gordon Rupp and Benjamin Drewery, Documents of Modern History (London: Arnold, 1970), 5–7.

Christians are walking displays of the nature of our God. He takes empty, dead, and darkened people and makes us alive, happy, and glorious in him. Isaiah writes that the Lord gives us beauty for ashes, the oil of gladness for mourning, and a garment of praise for our faint spirits. Once devastated, ruined cities, we become "oaks of righteousness," planted by God himself so that he may display in us his own glory and beauty in the world (61:3–4). Now born in Zion, we belong to the Lord and manifest his life in our own lives. The Christian life is, by its very nature, a testimony to the grace of God. In him, we have found a wholeness, healing, and happiness that are not simply for us to enjoy. Because this life is *his* gift—the gift of the ever-outgoing, generous God—it is a *godly* life that delights to multiply, spread out, and increase.

Glorified in Christ and being renewed in his image, believers become shining lights in the world, as he is *the* light of the world (Matt. 5:16; John 8:12), shining with his own light as we hold him out to "a crooked and twisted generation" (Phil. 2:14–16). Like scent diffusers, we spread "the fragrance of the knowledge of him," which is upon us in such a way that some will immediately savor the aroma of eternal life, and others the odor of judgment and death (2 Cor. 2:14–16), as though confronted with the Savior and Judge himself. Indeed, even as we "share his sufferings" (Phil. 3:10), we are "carrying in the body the death of Jesus, so that the life of Jesus may also be manifested in our bodies" (2 Cor. 4:10). We were once shrunken and grey, but now—even in suffering and self-denial—manifest and shine the life of God *outward*.

Cross-Shaped Living

If sinful humanity is curved in on itself, then redeemed humanity is, by nature, expansive and open. In Christ we become whole and overflowing—big-hearted and magnanimous in the image of God. We are amazed that the Lord finds joy in being kind to his people. "I will rejoice in doing them good, and I will plant them in this land in faithfulness, with all my heart and all my soul" (Jer. 32:41). His heart is truly in it as he is good to us: he is not grudging, and his treatment of us is not going against the grain in any way. Heartfelt and soulful, his very joy is in blessing us. And the soul that has drunk at this spring can only grow to be more like God: delighting to give, share, host, encourage, and bless.

For us, this way of being does, for now, go against the old grain. Our flesh will always tend toward smallness of soul, insularity, and selfishness. We will still, at times, be driven by fear and idolatry, seeking to control our lives and those around us. So long as we remain in the body and until the Lord returns, this sense of tension will be with us, and the two principles will be at war within. The mark of Christian integrity is not to deny that sin still lives in us (Rom. 7:17; 1 John 1:8) but to the join the battle daily, taking the old self to the cross.

At the foot of the cross, we are humbled again and again and shown our own natural emptiness, yet there we also fill our gaze afresh with the glorious self-giving of God in Christ. The cross resets our expectations and imaginations of him, showing us the reality of his kindness, so that we receive anew his love and grace into our emptiness. The ministry of the Holy Spirit here is to help us to live according to the new life that is ours in Jesus (Rom. 8:11). He assures us of our adoption, bringing us back from the brink of slipping into slavery and fear; he enables us to call on God as our own "Abba! Father!"; he assures us of our eternal inheritance in Christ (Rom. 8:14–17). This Spirit-filled life is the death of the sinful nature in us and our growth into the sonship we have received (Rom. 8:13–14), transforming us into the image of the Son.

The Christian life in the Spirit is a cruciform life, preferring others over ourselves (Rom. 12:10), giving over and above what is asked of us (Matt. 5:40), laying down our own lives for the sake of others (1 John 3:16). At the cross, we never mistake our fullness for something intrinsic to us that we can boast about to credit ourselves or hold back from others, as though it were fragile or in need of protection. Freely we have received, so freely we give (Matt. 10:8). Just as the cross reveals God to be full and glorious in love, humility, and blessing, so it creates Christians who are the same way. It makes mean souls into lavish souls.

Charles Spurgeon shines as an example of a cross-enlarged soul. Since childhood, he had been spiritually burdened, physically quite frail, and prone to lifelong depression and fear. Once he wrote, "My spirits were sunken so low that I could weep by the hour like a child, and yet I knew not what I wept for."[9] Still, having been converted as a teenager, he exercised a ministry that positively boomed with the goodness of God. In his public prayers, his compilation of a hymnbook, and especially his preaching, but even in the way he shook hands with his church family after services, he wanted to display the abundant life of God.[10] He would not stand for unfeeling praying or preaching, nor for pastors who gave off an air of disinterest in people.

His own private life speaks of a man notably generous with his money, almost childlike in his delight in the created world, sincerely interested in other people, and full of mischievous fun. William Williams, a hymnwriter and friend of Spurgeon's, related, "I have

---

9 Darrel Amundsen, "The Anguish and Agonies of Charles Spurgeon," in *Christian History*, issue 29, vol. 10, no. 1 (1991): 24.

10 C. H. Spurgeon, *An All-Round Ministry: Addresses to Ministers and Students* (London: Passmore & Alabaster, 1900), 188–91.

laughed more, I verily believe, when in his company than during all the rest of my life besides."[11] Yet Spurgeon was also emotionally sensitive; his personality was not so domineering as to crush the quiet or vulnerable around him. His hearty embrace of life and other people came not so much from natural disposition as it blossomed in the sunshine of the gospel of the "blessed" (or "happy") God (1 Tim. 1:11).[12] Spurgeon is evidence of the renewing, restorative power of Christ in broken and fragile human lives.

Our Glory

The glory of the Christian is always Jesus Christ and him crucified. "For what we proclaim is not ourselves, but Jesus Christ as Lord, with ourselves as your servants for Jesus's sake," says Paul in 2 Corinthians 4:5; and "far be it from me to boast except in the cross of our Lord Jesus Christ" (Gal. 6:14). Knowing that we are empty ones, now full of him, we always place Jesus himself at the foreground, rather than ourselves. It is Jesus we have to offer to the world, and not ourselves.

In fact, the glory displayed in us is most often displayed *in spite of us*, with God choosing to make himself in known in our weakness. Indeed, "we have this treasure in jars of clay, to show that the surpassing power belongs to God and not to us" (2 Cor. 4:7). Paul experienced the Lord's assurance "My grace is sufficient for you, for my power is made perfect in weakness," and he even chose to boast about his weaknesses in order to have the power of Christ rest on him (2 Cor. 12:9–11).

11 William Williams, *Personal Reminiscences of Charles Haddon Spurgeon* (London: Passmore & Alabaster, 1895), 62.

12 See Michael Reeves, *Spurgeon on the Christian Life: Alive in Christ* (Wheaton, IL: Crossway, 2018), 32.

This counterintuitive embrace of our own weakness and dependence is the way the glory of God will shine in and through us. Our own attempts to be impressive, whole, and strong in mission will actually only betray our fallen emptiness and selfishness: they are the work of theologians of glory. But theologians of the cross are filled with the radiance of God, unearned, unexpected, and unquenchable. Happiness, beauty, and humility flow from the lives of those who are restored in the image of God. We who are naturally like the Gentile outsiders Rahab, Babylon, Philistia, Tyre, and Cush can come to say with all the people of God in Zion,

> On God rests my salvation and my glory;
>> my mighty rock, my refuge is God. (Ps. 62:7)

The one who called himself "the life" (John 14:6) makes us more truly alive; he who is the Father's image and Glory shines upon us and make us radiant like himself; the God of outgoing, self-giving love opens our hearts to him and to the world. Christians become the images and ambassadors of Christ, magnanimous ones who find joy in reaching out. This transformation from our empty, fallen life to the glorious, truly human (Christlike!) life is at the heart of healthy mission.

6

Arise, Shine!

IF CHRISTIANS ARE RENEWED in the image of God, "born in Zion," and shining with the glory of the Lord, why does mission continue to be such a challenge for us?

Too often, we find ourselves fragile and timid in mission, propelled by a mixed bag of motivations and emotions. We may be totally committed to mission as an activity of the church but feel low on energy and enthusiasm. We know that despite everything being right in theory, something is still missing, and we are simply not sparkling with the beauty and goodness of Jesus. While we know God to be full, our mission feels empty. What is going on?

How to Be a Bad Missionary

John and Charles Wesley were students at Oxford University in the 1720s. After some time spent in riotous living (which Charles referred to coyly as "diversions"), the brothers set up a Christian reading group with a friend. Three or four evenings a week, they would meet to read the Greek New Testament and books on the spiritual life by William Law and Thomas à Kempis. Their group, mocked by fellow students as "the Holy Club" and the "Bible-moths," soon grew to twenty or more members, including a young George Whitefield.

These earnest young men took food to poor families, visited those in the Castle Prison, and taught local orphans to read. On Wednesdays and Fridays, they would often fast until three in the afternoon. It was a powerhouse of piety, attention to spirituality, and service to the community. So it was no surprise that once the Wesley brothers had graduated, they decided to depart to Savannah, Georgia, in the United States, as missionaries. They set off in October 1735 full of youthful vigor and zeal.

On paper, they were the ultimate missionaries. They'd proved their devotion, bravely withstood ridicule and mockery, and were clearly willing to give up everything in obedience to God's call. But their trip was a disaster. Their High Church Anglican theology was not well-received, John was the subject of legal action, and Charles received heavy hints that he should consider a job in England. By the end of 1736, Charles had returned home, and John followed about a year later. Both were burned-out, ill, and depressed. Each felt that, spiritually, all was not well.

Living in London, desperate and discouraged, the brothers recalled a group of Moravian Christians they had met on their travels. They had watched amazed as this group prayed and sang hymns with a remarkable, deep peace during a savage storm at sea. For all the spiritual discipline and religious energy of the Holy Club, there was, in those Christians, something the Wesleys did not know and wanted to find. As they investigated this, they were introduced to the writings of Martin Luther and, for the first time, heard that God accepts sinners on account of their faith alone and not their works. This changed everything for the brothers, for, like Luther himself, it was the very reality check they had needed. Until then, they had only conceived of a God who needed their goodness in order to save them. A friend of Charles's had once asked him how he hoped to be saved, and Charles had replied, "Because I have used my best endeavors to serve God."[1] A God who freely justified sinners out of pure, undeserved grace was astonishing news to John and Charles. Wonderfully, in 1738, on the day of Pentecost, Charles was born again, at last finding "peace with God."[2] Three days later, John was also converted, famously writing in his diary of how his "heart strangely warmed" as he came to "trust in Christ, Christ alone for salvation"; he continued, "an assurance was given me that he had taken away my sins, even mine, and saved me from the law of sin and death."[3]

As much as the brothers had committed themselves to a strict lifestyle of outward holiness and study of the Scriptures, and even as they crossed the ocean to be missionaries, they had never truly known the glorious love of God in Christ. Their ministry and mission were not the fruit of happy hearts but the toil of spiritual captives.

Jesus reproved the religious leaders of his day for exactly this distortion of mission work:

But woe to you, scribes and Pharisees, hypocrites! For you shut the kingdom of heaven in people's faces. For you neither enter yourselves nor allow those who would enter to go in. Woe to you, scribes and Pharisees, hypocrites! For you travel across sea and land to make a single proselyte, and when he becomes a proselyte, you make him twice as much a child of hell as yourselves. (Matt. 23:13–15)

There is much to see here. The scribes and Pharisees belonged not to the kingdom of heaven but to hell, and they willingly went great

1   Arnold A. Dallimore, *A Heart Set Free: The Life of Charles Wesley* (Wheaton, IL: Crossway, 1988), 58–59.
2   Dallimore, *A Heart Set Free*, 61.
3   John Wesley, *The Works of John Wesley: The Bicentennial Edition*, ed. W. Reginald Ward and Richard P. Heitzenrater, vol. 18 (Nashville: Abingdon, 1988), 249–50.

distances for their "mission." They prevented people from hearing the true gospel and recruited them into a life that Jesus had already described as hypocrisy (Matt. 23:3). Notice that Jesus referred to their fruit not as "converts" but as "proselytes." Self-justifying, empire-building evangelists may see many proselytes won by force of personality or impressive communication, but hypocrites can only give birth to hypocrites. These are converts not to the gospel of Christ but to another gospel.

This is the very definition of "empty" mission—and it begins with a tragically thin view of God. The Pharisees were theologians of glory, doing "all their deeds to be seen by others" (Matt. 23:5). They sought the praise and glory of people rather than of God. Without assurance of the Lord's free grace and love, they were insecure and petty (Matt. 12:2), willing to climb over others for attention, praying ostentatiously in public places, and comparing themselves with one another (Matt. 6:5; Luke 18:11). Theirs was a world of underhanded scheming (Matt. 22:15) and fear (John 7:13; 20:19), so that Nicodemus had to meet Jesus under cover of darkness (John 3:2). Pharisees cannot truly love God or other people, because they have not first enjoyed the love of God for themselves. When disciples of an empty, demanding God do mission, they will tend to be results-driven bullies.

Even an evangelist who *preaches* a gospel of grace but is really justifying himself betrays the fact that God seems to him neither near nor kind—not truly gracious or glorious. And by his fruit we will know him, because he will be just the same as his god (Matt. 7:20).

Sticks and Carrots

When Christians are not filled to overflowing with the glorious goodness of God, mission is not a natural or comfortable thing, and we will have to find other motivations to drive them. Church leaders who are persuaded that the church *ought* to be missional are left scratching their heads trying to mobilize congregations that seem reticent and unenthused. The most tempting solution at this point is not to deal with the underlying theological issue but to unveil a practical training program or to teach strongly about the reasons Christians *should* evangelize. Many biblical reasons, of course, can be listed—all quite correctly—but the pastor frustrated with a recalcitrant flock is always in peril of dealing only with the surface issues. And frequently he will turn for help to the sinister twins: duty and debt.

It is not uncommon to hear conference speakers or youth leaders in drill sergeant mode, firing up their listeners with what amounts to little more than a guilt trip. The Christian duty is to "go into all the world," we are told, and only lazy, selfish believers have not already promised the Lord they will go anywhere, anytime if he calls. Since Jesus has done so much for you, how could you refuse him?

There is no doubt that the great need of the world must shake the church into action, but the only hearts that will be genuinely moved with compassion for the lost are hearts that have enjoyed mercy themselves (Luke 6:36). Christians *can* be cajoled into evangelism like a herd of animals, but this is not a foundation for healthy and effective mission. In fact, it only *looks like* evangelism, for here our leaders—and God himself—end up seeming as intimidating as the task of reaching the world. Christians who are only scolded for their lack of commitment and sent packing to the mission field are not gladly overflowing ambassadors but Pharisees. Duty and debt are cruel motivations for mission. Those who try to draw on them will end up unconvinced salespeople who peddle a product they do not finally believe in or enjoy for themselves.

What about the reality of eternity: resurrection and judgment, heaven and hell? Surely the biblical teaching about the wrath of God against sin and the fate of the unsaved would be like smelling salts to lethargic Christians, snapping us into action, wouldn't they? It is true that our love for our unbelieving family members and acquaintances must lead us to hold out Christ to them as well as to regular prayer for their salvation. The predicament of unreached people groups may stir in some of us the desire to go abroad and devote ourselves to preaching the gospel where it is not yet known. In such compassion, mixed with urgency, we are surely sampling and imitating the love of God for the world, as he is "patient toward you, not wishing that any should perish, but that all should reach repentance" (2 Pet. 3:9). Yet, ultimately, it is not *hell* that propels us. Judgment is real and we must never shirk from teaching congregations honestly about it in missions, but it is not in itself the *primary* logic for evangelism.

Evangelism is, by definition, the good news of Christ, not only a warning about the last day. When it comes to motivating Christians to mission, the gospel that moves the missionary must be the same one he or she expects to win the hearts of the lost. If we burden Christians with the guilt of abandoning people to hell, it will be the message of guilt and hell they will pass on, rather than the message of the Savior of sinners and conqueror of hell. Jesus Christ will not be *the jewel* of the gospel they tell, but only *the means* to escape a terrible end. Not only this, but the resulting converts will have been motivated by their preexisting instinct for self-preservation. Disciples who are won not by the glory of the Lord to repentance and faith but by an appeal to their own well-being will continue in exactly the same direction. Their newfound faith will be more about themselves than about Christ.

Deeper still, at the root of all these motivations is an undelightful god. A god who keeps a record of our debts, accepts us in proportion to our performance, and is primarily a threat to us will never be the star attraction of our message. We are likely to cut him out of the equation where possible. Every god has some "mission," and every god is advertised by his followers one way or another, for his qualities, values, and character are worked out in all their words and deeds. But unless Christians are carried into mission by genuine enjoyment of the Lord, their mission will not embody the glory of the living God.

There are also rewards we might set before Christians to engage them in mission. The carrot is mightier than the stick. We might dwell on the capacity of evangelism to deepen our own growth and sanctification. It is true that when we step out and share the gospel with others it does very often have the effect of building us up in confidence and spiritual maturity. Many of us have had the sense of the Holy Spirit guiding our words and questions in such conversations as we turn to the Scriptures or relate our experience of knowing Jesus. Often our friends are more receptive than we might have imagined, and we come away feeling strangely lifted and (if we dare admit it) a little surprised that the gospel actually works. By the Lord's providence, these experiences can strengthen our conviction and boost our development as disciples. As well as personal growth, we might mention the importance of mission in the life of any Christian who would desire any responsibility or leadership role in the life of the church. The young believer who would like to become a small group leader or help with children's work might well be asked when she last spoke to a friend about her faith or led someone to the Lord. Mission experience is seen as a valuable item on the résumé of any Christian ambitious to serve or lead.

Now, discovering someone's attitude toward evangelism may well be a useful diagnostic tool in sensing that person's maturity. Yet, in these "reward" scenarios, we risk communicating to people that mission is part of a conditional relationship with God and his church.

"*If* you prove your zeal and commitment by helping get the message out and grow our church, *then* we can let you play in the worship team/preach/lead a ministry like you always wanted." Mission may become a transactional activity, undertaken not out of uninhibited love for the Lord and the lost but, once again, from love of self. Some will back out of the deal, withdrawing to more comfortable and less demanding corners of the church; the more resilient may steel themselves to do what has been asked of them. Either way, mission becomes a means to the wrong end.

In the long run, even "carrots" do not work as ultimate motivations for mission. They are, by nature, *additions* to what believers already have in knowing God. Offering sweeteners in the deal to entice Christians into action communicates to them that mission is something fundamentally *other* than, and *extra* to, knowing God and overflowing with *that* enjoyment. You know God already, we imply, but there are additional benefits for you to collect if you'll play the game. This cannot be the primary way the church fuels its mission. Instead, there must be a "further up and further in" here, because happy mission is rooted not in our response to God, nor even in better understanding God's plans and purposes, but in *his own nature*. The truest and highest motivation for mission is God himself.

Cutting Out Christ

If we are not captured specifically by the glory of God in Christ and propelled outward in happy proclamation of the one who has freely given himself to us, then it will be no surprise when our message quickly has little to do with him. If it is not *him* we are enjoying, it will not be *him* we convey to others. Even unwittingly, we may become ministers of another gospel (Gal. 1:7). It may not be the out-and-out false gospels of, for example, prosperity or "health and wealth," but something more subtle. Our tendency will be toward abstraction from God, focusing on things that, almost without our notice, are not quite Jesus Christ and him crucified. We may find ourselves emphasizing themes of the gospel like "grace" or "heaven" but not explicitly holding out *Christ* as the gift and as the treasure of heaven. We may offer the world the hope of transformed lives, healed hurts, and renewed communities, but make Jesus the *means* to these things rather than the center of them all. These things are blessings of the gospel, but if they are elevated to become its center and our focus, they will become nothing more than substitute gods.

Of course, sometimes our attempts to correct our own faulty thinking can cause us to overbalance. As in many areas of church life, we can be too easily driven by reacting to some error or omission we have spotted and allow *it* to shape what we do and say more than the Scriptures and their presentation of Christ.

In the twentieth century, theologians and missiologists recognized that for too long "mission" had been seen as the preserve only of specially called individuals who crossed the sea to reach the unreached. Scholars began to speak of the *missio ecclesiae* (the mission or "sending" of the church) as an extension of, and participation in, the *missio Dei* (the mission of God). The idea of the *missio Dei* captures the idea that God has a grand purpose in the world, that the Father *sends* and the Son and Spirit *go*. This divine mission is really the logic and bedrock of human mission as the church is sent into the world with the gospel.[4] The idea of *missio Dei* is helpful in reminding us that what the church does in preaching the gospel and reaching out to the world is not our independent activity. This concept rightly

---

4 For the classic summary, see David J. Bosch, *Transforming Mission: Paradigm Shifts in Theology of Mission*, 20th anniversary ed. (Maryknoll, NY: Orbis, 2011), 9–10.

shows that the whole dynamic of sending and going is derived from the life of the triune God, rather than being a separate and secondary churchly activity in response. God's action and gracious initiative long precede ours.

These are good foundations, but some proponents of the idea have drifted into abstraction. If the mission of God is broader and wider than that of the church, they suggest, it may be that we must concede that God is doing things in the world that have nothing to do with the church or perhaps even *exclude* the church.[5] So, while we might have been handed the well-defined task of preaching the gospel, God himself could be equally interested in almost anything that we might consider good for the world or that promotes the flourishing of humankind. From combating world poverty to reducing carbon emissions, anything could be part of God's mission in just as essential a way as the good news of Jesus.

The danger here is trying to discern what God might be doing beyond what he has explicitly revealed about his purposes for the church and her bridegroom. Where Christians have begun to accept this, there has inevitably been a decline in straightforward proclamation evangelism. Of course, feeding the hungry and stewarding the created world are as good and biblical as grace and heaven. They are, without question, things that Christians and churches should be involved in. Ministries of mercy and compassion are necessary to express true Christian character; they adorn the gospel (1 Thess. 2:8), proving our faith to be living and fruitful (James 2:14). But they are not the *content* of the gospel, nor finally the thing we have to offer to the world. Generosity with financial and practical resources and

5   See Bosch, *Transforming Mission*, 398–401.

commitment to the good of the earth are not qualities that Christians alone possess; they are not the church's "unique selling point" or the focal point of our mission in the world. Proclaiming Christ and doing good are not even equal partners in this sense: God's mission is revealed in the sending of his Son, and the church is sent with the mission of heralding that same Son. Because of this, the proclamation of the gospel, the heralding of Christ, is the nonnegotiable of mission.

This means that slipping into casual conversation with a colleague that you happened to go to church on weekends may be a good and helpful conversation starter, but in itself it is not shining with the glory of God. Being a kind and decent person and hoping that others might see a difference in you is part and parcel of being a Christian but in itself is not yet evangelism. Evangelism has *content* to it, and the content is Jesus Christ himself. In other words, our offering to the world is not ourselves but the Lord. We are not simply imitators of him but participants, conveyors, carriers of his word and his glory.

Martin Luther is among a number of theologians who identify God's word as having three forms: it is, first, Christ, the Word of the Father (John 1:1); second, the Scriptures, the Spirit-breathed word of Christ, which speak of him (Col. 3:16); and, third, the preaching of the church. At first, this seems a strange idea. How can the feeble words of preachers and evangelists *be* the word of God? Yet, as Paul says to the Thessalonians, "When you received the word of God, which you heard from us, you accepted it not as the word of men *but as what it really is, the word of God*" (1 Thess. 2:13). The writer to the Hebrews, similarly, exhorts his readers, "Remember your leaders, those who spoke to you *the word of God*" (13:7). When we proclaim Christ the Word from the scriptural word, it is "*him* we proclaim" (Col. 1:28). To the Corinthians, Paul said: "We are ambassadors for Christ, *God making his appeal through us. We implore you on behalf of Christ*, be reconciled to God" (2 Cor. 5:20). Luther, reflecting on all this, and preaching on John 20, where Jesus appears to give his disciples authority to forgive the sins of others, says:

> It is a great and excellent thing for the mouth of every honest minister and preacher to be Christ's mouth, and his word and forgiveness to be Christ's word and forgiveness. If you sin and confess it, believing on Christ, then your minister and preacher will forgive you the same sin in Christ's place, and the words which he speaks on God's behalf you ought to accept as if Christ himself had spoken them to you. Therefore, it is right to call the word of the minister and preacher which he preaches God's word, for the office is not the minister's and the preacher's, but God's; and the word that he preaches is likewise not the minister's and preacher's, but God's.[6]

Here is a bold and brilliant vision of the way the church very literally holds out Christ. With his word on our lips, the living Word is made known through us, speaking, enlightening, and drawing the world to himself. In a Christmas sermon on Luke 2:14–20, Luther pushes the implications of this theology of the word:

> The word he speaks within himself and which remains within him, is never separated from him. . . . His word is not merely an exhalation or a noise, but carries with it the whole essence of the divine nature and, as we said above in the Epistle where we dealt with brightness of his glory and image, divine nature is formed to accompany the image and it becomes the very image itself. The brilliance also radiates the glory so that it merges with the glory.

---

6   Martin Luther, sermon on John 20:19–31 (1533), in Eugene F. A. Klug, *Sermons of Martin Luther: The House Postils*, vol. 2 (Grand Rapids, MI: Baker, 1996), 56.

. . . Behold, here we see the source of the apostle's words when he calls Christ an image of the divine essence and a brightness of divine glory.[7]

The Word of God is no mere breath or sound but the exact expression of his Father, "the essence of the divine nature." The one who is the radiance of the glory of God *is* the outshining of the image of the Father. God's communication of himself *is* himself in his Son. Jesus the Word of God spoken to us in the incarnation, in Scripture, and in the church's proclamation *is God with us*. This could not be more astounding. In the word of God, even when it is spoken by fallible and sinful humans, God truly gives *himself*. This means that in our proclamation of Christ in sermons, evangelistic messages, and even conversations about the gospel, Christ the Word is present in power. God is speaking his own Word; God is enlightening with his own light; God is offering *himself* to those who hear. Richard Sibbes, writing of the angels' acclamation at the Nativity, explained:

> Light is a glorious creature. Nothing expresseth glory so much as light. It is a sweet creature, but it is a glorious creature. It carries its evidence in itself, it discovers all other things and itself too. So excellency and eminency will discover itself to those that have eyes to see it; and being manifested, and withal taken notice of, is glory.[8]

This is why the biblical writers are so convinced that there is power in proclamation: that the gospel is the very "power of God" (Rom. 1:16); that the word we hear at our conversion from a man in a pulpit or a prayerful, witnessing mother is actually "imperishable seed"

---

7 Martin Luther, sermon on Luke 2:14–20, in *Luther's Works*, vol. 52, *Sermons II*, ed. Hans J. Hillerbrand and Helmut T. Lehmann (Philadelphia: Fortress; St. Louis, MO: Concordia, 1974), 45.

8 Richard Sibbes, *The Complete Works of Richard Sibbes*, ed. Alexander B. Grosart, vol. 6 (Edinburgh: Nichol, 1862), 34–35.

(1 Pet. 1:23); that the light of Christ shining in our hearts is nothing other than the light of God who first said, "Let there be light" in the universe (2 Cor. 4:6). When we go out with the gospel, we are holding in our hands "the power of God" (Rom. 1:16). Preaching *Christ* and not ourselves (2 Cor. 4:5), our personal stories, our experiences, or our perspectives, we bring God himself to bear on the lives of our hearers.

At times in her proclamation of the gospel, the church has slipped into an oversimplified gospel that has only to do with sin and salvation, missing the biblical emphasis on God's good creation and his promise to re-create the heavens and the earth in the end. We may present the gospel in terms of "fall and redemption" in such a way that we veer into a rather gnostic disregard for the body, the created world, and the state of things until Jesus's return. Concerned with "saving souls," we have given the impression that Christianity is simply securing a ticket to heaven and that our lives and societies now are finally irrelevant. This is not a thoroughgoing, biblical point of view. A number of theologians and pastors have attempted to recapture the fuller biblical story of creation, fall, redemption, and renewal, mining not just Genesis 3 to Romans 3, but Genesis 1 to Revelation 22. God's original design for humanity was not only to "repent!" but to "be fruitful!" (Gen. 1:28), and it is for this that we are redeemed in Jesus. Christians are a part of God's grand purpose to renew all things in his Son. Again, there is helpful correction here. Yet we must also be careful with our language. We must also be clear on *how* Scripture tells us that God renews all things and how believers take part in that.

One pitfall here is to overemphasize the production and transformation of culture as the *means* of renewal. The Christian life has sometimes been cast in terms of Jeremiah's call to the exiles to "seek the welfare of the city where I [the LORD] have sent you into exile, and pray to the LORD on its behalf, for in its welfare you will find your welfare" (Jer. 29:7). We join God in the renewal of all things, some say, as we go into our communities to teach children, start charities, create beautiful art, and engage in politics. Participating fully and faithfully in the various spheres of society, we transform culture in Jesus's name. In this way, we display something of the fullness of redeemed humanity, skillfully and heartily pursuing God-glorifying excellence like the craftsmen Bezalel and Oholiab (Ex. 31:1–6).

But simply doing things well (or even distinctively) in our various spheres is not the full extent of our calling as Christians. Scripture consistently makes the *proclamation of Christ* the means of God's work in people and in the whole creation. It is not primarily human *culture* that God is renewing but human *beings*, in his Son, who became one of us. Of course, the renewal of culture will seem like an exciting calling in big cities full of young people working in nonprofits, education, the arts, or as baristas, whose lives and livelihoods are cultural contributions. Yet the mission of the church is for all Christians and must make sense to the factory production-line worker, the sleepless single mother, the unemployed, and the homeless. While not everybody can consider himself or herself a society shaper or culture maker, there is no Christian who cannot share the love of Jesus with another person. This is the renewal work to which God has called each of us. We are to be the embodiment not primarily of "the good life" but of *Christ*, in our deeds but also in our words. We can and must tell the full story of God's purposes in the world, but we must *tell* the story.

Again, pushing against the gnostic drift, some have spoken of the importance of mission being "incarnational." Rather than bombing our neighborhoods with gospel tracts and then shutting ourselves up safely in our churches to pray for revival "out there," the church must embody the gospel. Just as Christ came into the world to save sinners (1 Tim. 1:15), so we are to proclaim Christ in a Christlike way: involved, in person, in relationships, and available. This emphasis captures the example of the early Christians who gave themselves wholly to the communities they cared for (1 Thess. 2:9–12), but a snare lies here if we begin to confuse ourselves with the content of the gospel. We may wonder: Have we involved ourselves sufficiently, invested enough, or commended the gospel as faithfully as we could? Might our Christlikeness be mission's success, or our inconsistency its ruin?

We need to exercise care here. The incarnation we must hold out to the world is *Christ's* and not our own. We rightly do this "in the world" though not "of the world" (John 17:11), but our full-throated humanity must only ever be a witness to *his* in its saving power. And we must never fear that our unavoidable failures to be truly human can undo the seeds of truth we plant. The gospel *is* the power of God (Rom. 1:16), and it does not need us to be its guardians and protectors. As much as Paul describes his ministry in relational language as motherly (1 Thess. 2:7), fatherly (1 Thess. 2:11), and a personal example of holiness (1 Thess. 2:10), these are descriptions of the quality of his main activity: proclaiming the gospel of God (1 Thess. 2:9). Paul sees this proclamation as the key to his ministry because the gospel, not Paul himself, has divine power: it is *the word of God* that is "at work" in the believers (1 Thess. 2:13).

Sidelined by Strategy

Another way we may fall into empty mission is to focus our attention more squarely on our strategy for outreach than on knowing God and sharing his life with the world. We may pour our time and energy into refuting the latest broadside from the new atheists or dismantling the assumptions of postmodernism and post-structuralism without filling our hearts and minds with the gospel of Christ each day. This is the perennial temptation of any who would study theology or apologetics—to become "professional" in information and arguments *about* God while neglecting communion with him. Dealing constantly with systems of thought and belief can quickly be a distraction from dealing with real persons, whether human or divine. In *The Great Divorce*, Lewis's mentor warns:

> There have been men before now who got so interested in proving the existence of God that they came to care nothing for God Himself . . . as if the good Lord had nothing to do but exist! There have been some who were so occupied in spreading Christianity that they never gave a thought to Christ. Man! Ye see it in smaller matters. Did ye never know a lover of books that with all his first editions and signed copies had lost the power to read them? Or an organiser of charities that had lost all love for the poor? It is the subtlest of all the snares.[9]

It may be that we recognize something of this in ourselves. We might relish the idea of winning an argument or a skirmish in the "culture war" more than we savor intimacy with God. Like the Pharisees, we are likely to become activist and aggressive in our methods. Our mission will be mercenary, seeing people as "projects" or "conquests." What we feature on our business cards and social media profiles may not be what actually governs our lives. Tellingly, even non-Christians can sometimes identify this. The evangelist

9   C. S. Lewis, *The Great Divorce* (London: Bles, 1946; repr., London: Collins, 2015), 74.

Glen Scrivener reports a comment made by a Western Buddhist correspondent in response to stories of scandals involving Christian ministers:

> The amount of time, money, ingenuity, effort, and sacrifices Christians expend to convert others is truly astonishing. You pray for it, have conferences on how to do it, celebrate it when it's successful, vow to keep trying when it isn't, donate money for it. Even the many admirable projects Christians have to help the sick and marginalized often have a conversion agenda behind them.
>
> Could Christians suffer fewer scandals if they paid less attention to converting others and more to transforming themselves? Might their time be better spent teaching congregations to develop self-awareness than encouraging them to evangelize their neighbours?
>
> Could it be that the imperative to convert others is really an unconscious strategy to avoid looking at oneself? . . . I'm sure [Christian ministers at the center of scandals] started out as sincere Christians but I'm just as sure the need to fulfil the great commission led them to make compromises . . . then exaggerating, then becoming a good actor, then becoming blind to their personal issues—pride, lust for power, sexual desire, etc. They had no time to look at themselves; they were too busy planning how to save others.[10]

While the commenter would clearly prefer a world in which Christians did not seek to convert others at all—something we cannot agree with—these comments have rightly identified the rot that can

---

10   Private email to Glen Scrivener (@glenscrivener), "Recently a Buddhist listener to the LIVEcast wrote in," Twitter, May 4, 2021, 11:56 a.m., https://twitter.com/glenscrivener/status/138960 9913865883654. Shared with the commenter's permission.

set in very accurately. We can very gradually sacrifice the quality of our "inner life" for the sake of "success" in ministry and mission. Not satisfied in the Lord, we use mission, and even those we try to reach, to fill our own emptiness. This may take the form of lying about the number of people who "prayed the prayer" after our sermons to make us look good, racking up speaking engagements to show ourselves worthy, or betraying the trust of vulnerable seekers who confide in us. We may even convince ourselves that our compromises with slowly mounting sin, spiritual dryness, and hypocrisy are somehow excusable and inevitable in a work as strategically vital as ours. We come to imagine that while we might sometimes do things that God disapproves of, fundamentally he *needs* us and is grateful to have us on his team. An empty god ruling over an empty church will only empty out the subjects of its mission: using and abusing, dehumanizing and destroying.

The God We Know Is the God We Show

If God seems to us to be empty and needy, we will serve him with empty hearts, finally taking what we need from the world rather than freely blessing it. What we truly worship and cherish will, for good or ill, be revealed in our mission. It is possible to look completely theologically orthodox while doing this kind of mission. We may doggedly cling to the inerrancy of Scripture, the uniqueness of Christ, the doctrine of hell, and substitutionary atonement while—all the while—exposing the world to an *undelightful* God. The God we know—or think we know—is the God we will show to the world. If we ourselves do not constantly revel in his free justification of sinners, his self-giving love, and his Son poured out to death for us while we were still his enemies, then we will be ghostly, unhappy Christians holding out a black hole of a god to people already dying.

Having spiritual life is vitally important, but simply being born again does not guarantee spiritual vitality and fruitfulness in mission. It is essential for our own hearts and for our witness that we have a right knowledge of God: that we are ever deepening in our appreciation of his goodness and constantly refreshed in his kindness. Even the truly regenerate will fall into spiritual ill-health if they allow their knowledge of God to stagnate and become domesticated. When we come to Scripture and have our minds renewed in the truth of God, we will find not only our own thinking corrected and realigned, but also our proclamation beautified and sharpened.

Jonathan Edwards is famous for his sermon "Sinners in the Hands of an Angry God," preached in 1741. It is an unflinching exposition of the danger of hell for the unconverted. A few years later, he was struck by a conversation with his friend David Brainerd. Brainerd had been preaching the gospel to Indians in New Jersey and reported, "It was surprising to see how their hearts seemed to be pierced with the tender and melting invitations of the Gospel, when there was not a word of terror spoken to them."[11]

Brainerd's experience convinced Edwards that people could be converted even without the threat of judgment provoking them to fear. They needed to hear about *God* as the first and greatest priority. The glory of God in Christ was sufficient and powerful to draw unbelievers to repentance and faith. Of course, Edwards was not wrong to preach "Sinners in the Hands of an Angry God," and he never turned his back on preaching judgment, but his growing desire was to have his preaching filled with the glory of God. After Brainerd died in 1747 and Edwards began his biography, his own works were increasingly marked

---

11 Jonathan Edwards, *The Works of Jonathan Edwards*, vol. 7, *The Life of David Brainerd*, ed. Norman Pettit (New Haven, CT: Yale University Press, 1985), 307.

by an even sharper focus on God's glory and beauty.[12] As his knowledge of God was deepened, his mission and ministry were enriched.

Real, fruitful, healthy mission must begin with delight in God. This absolutely relies on orthodoxy (believing rightly), but simply affirming truths cannot guarantee it. Our hearts must be filled with the glory of God in Christ. His glory, more than simply boasting splendor and strength, exudes joy and beauty, awakening joy in us and fertilizing our proclamation of him. As one theologian has put it:

> God is glorious in such a way that He radiates joy, so that He is all He is with and not without beauty. Otherwise His glory might well be joyless. And if a different view of His glory is taken and taught, then even with the best will in the world, and even with the greatest seriousness and zeal, the proclamation of His glory will always have in a slight or dangerous degree something joyless, without sparkle or humour, not to say tedious and therefore finally neither persuasive nor convincing.[13]

Indeed, empty mission might look to Jesus in his glory, beauty, humanity, and self-giving and simply conclude that we must go away and be more like him. But full and fulfilled mission recognizes that we become more like him—transformed *by* and *into* his glory—precisely as we look on him, know him more truly, and delight ourselves in him (2 Cor. 3:18). We become like the one we worship. His happiness makes us happy; his kindness makes us kind; his glory fills us. Then, made beautiful like our Lord, with compassion and verve we will carry the blessing of Jesus to the ends of the earth.

---

12 See, for example, "The End for Which God Created the World"; see also our chap. 8.
13 Karl Barth, *Church Dogmatics II/1: The Doctrine of God*, pt. 1 (1957; repr., Peabody, MA: Hendrickson, 2010), 655.

When Isaiah called the people of Israel to "arise, shine," it was because "your light has come, and *the glory of the LORD has risen upon you*" (60:1). This was no frustrated outburst, pushing them to "get up and jolly well get on with it," but a promise that, amid the darkness covering the world, "his glory will be seen upon you" (60:2). The Lord himself was to be with them, enlightening (60:3), enriching (60:5), and beautifying (60:9) them. As God shines upon his beloved redeemed people (60:16), so he will shine *out from* us.

7

Those Who Look to
Him Are Radiant

WHAT MAKES FOR HEALTHY, FRUITFUL MISSION? A crack team of highly driven extraverts charming seekers into the kingdom? Slick church services that ooze cultural relevance and credibility? Genius programs and courses that make space for questions while delivering the gospel with sensitivity?

The foundation of all our mission is our knowledge and enjoyment of God. Yes, I may be born again, but I may not yet be a good missionary. I may have the right intellectual conviction about God's goodness but be unmoved by him. I may know just what to say and how to say it in my gospel presentation, honoring the Lord with my lips while remaining far from him in my heart (Isa. 29:13).

Our delight in God is the main fuel for mission.

When we find ourselves struggling with motivation, battling against guilt, or discouraged with the fruit of our witness, we must return to the cross, where the fountain of God's goodness is opened to us. When our evangelism becomes dry and dutiful, we must come for our hearts' refreshment to Jesus, who shows us the reality of his

Father in heaven. Those who would be happy missionaries must know and delight in God. This means that missionaries need to become theologians all over again. All who would proclaim Christ and his gospel must regularly, obsessively, and joyfully come to the gracious self-revelation of God in Christ if they are to be good missionaries.

A Good Theologian Is a Good Missionary

John Calvin knew well the vital union between knowing God and mission. Calvin is known primarily as a theologian and Bible commentator and was notoriously quiet and bookish, even physically fragile. But Calvin married all this with a less well-known missionary flare. In Geneva, where he ministered, he set up a school of theology, known as the Academy, to train up the next generation of pastors. His aim wasn't simply to give his students a theological education but to send them out all over the world in mission. In fact, his plan was to raise and deploy theologically educated missionary ministers *from* all over Europe *to* all of Europe and even beyond. He saw that the truths the Reformation had freshly rediscovered had to be trumpeted across the continent.

The strategy worked brilliantly, with missionaries going out beyond Europe, even as far as Brazil. Calvin was a Frenchman, and from his base in Geneva he paid special attention to his homeland, which was no safe place for evangelical believers. Between 1555 and 1562, around a hundred missionaries were sent into France, ready to preach and evangelize, equipped with miniature Bibles and flat-pack communion sets that could be hidden in the lining of their clothes. In the end, more than two thousand congregations made up of around three million members were established in France through the efforts of around fifteen hundred students from the

Geneva Academy.[1] This was a theological seminary simultaneously functioning as a high-octane church-planting operation with its sights set on the most hostile territory.

What was behind this bold strategy and wonderful fruitfulness? Calvin's students set out with evangelistic zeal *because of the theological foundation they received.* As Daniel 11:32 has it, the people who will "stand firm and take action" are those who *"know their God."* Calvin "believed that a good missionary had to be a good theologian first."[2] Indeed, a good theologian is a good missionary, *and* a good missionary is a good theologian. This was not to make mission the realm of experts and academics: the knowledge of God is available to all in the Scriptures. Rather, Calvin saw that those people who knew God most deeply and satisfyingly would be the best at winning hearts into the kingdom; and those most thrilled at the prospect of taking the gospel out into the world were those most captured by the beauty and goodness of the God of the gospel.

The inner logic of this can be seen in Calvin's most famous work, *Institutes of the Christian Religion.* Designed as an introduction to the Christian faith (*institutio* means "instruction"), the *Institutes* went through a number of editions and was smuggled into France alongside the Scriptures as an evangelistic and pastoral resource. The work is split into four "books": *The Knowledge of God the Creator, The Knowledge of God the Redeemer in Christ, The Way in Which We Receive the Grace of Christ,* and *The External Means or Aids by Which God Invites Us into the Society of Christ and Holds Us Therein.* In these

---

1 W. Stanford Reid, "Calvin's Geneva: A Missionary Centre," *The Reformed Theological Review* 42, no. 3 (1983): 69. See also Michael A. G. Haykin and C. Jeffrey Robinson Sr., *To the Ends of the Earth: Calvin's Missional Vision and Legacy* (Wheaton, IL: Crossway, 2014).

2 Frank A. James III, "Calvin the Evangelist," *Reformed Quarterly* 19, no. 2 (2001): 8.

four books, Calvin wanted to cover all the bases of Christian doctrine and Christian living ("the Sum of Piety") and, following the structure of the Apostles' Creed, all that we learn in the *Institutes* buds and flowers from the knowledge of God. Books 3 and 4 of the *Institutes*, which deal with everything from the Christian attitude toward food and money to prayer to church government, could never come before books 1 and 2 in Calvin's world. Nothing in the Christian life can be abstracted or detached from knowing God; everything can be appreciated properly only when we see it in relation to him.

Calvin famously opens the *Institutes* by saying that even our knowledge of ourselves (which we might think of as home turf) cannot be certain and clear without first knowing God. The great gifts and abilities that humanity possesses are "benefits shed like dew from heaven upon us" and cannot be explained and understood without allowing them to lead us "as by rivulets to the spring itself."[3] Calvin intended the very structure of the *Institutes* to show that *from* our knowledge of God as Creator and Redeemer flows all the practice and outworking of the Christian faith in our lives.

A Geneva Academy student, slipping over the border into darkest France to begin a dangerous and challenging ministry, would have had it drilled into him that *knowing God* was to be his first and most essential priority. The fact that God had purposes in the world, or that God had called him to participate in them, or that the lost really must be won was not enough. Only knowing God could fill him up and send him out, rousing and sustaining his mission. Only a deep and rich knowledge of God could keep his heart full and his head up as he took his life in his hands. The same goes for

---

3   John Calvin, *Institutes of the Christian Religion*, ed. John T. McNeill, trans. Ford Lewis Battles (Philadelphia: Westminster, 1960), 1.1.1–2.

anyone who would go out with the gospel today. Considering the contours of the biblical narrative of God's mission is of great value. Knowing the history of the church's missionary efforts is inspiring. Understanding the latest theory and literature in missiology is enriching. But beneath all these is the irreplaceable foundation of knowing and enjoying God.

This is nothing more than the teaching of Jesus in John 15, who calls his disciples to abide in him, "the true vine," if they would bear fruit (vv. 1–4). The only fruitful branches on the vine are those which abide in him, or specifically abide *in his love* (v. 9). Branches that do not abide in him wither and die (v. 6), proving themselves never to have been truly a part of him. But living in Christ's love will mean his own joy will fill us (v. 11). Fruitful mission is certainly an activity: it requires going out and speaking up, and yet it can only be as the *fruit* of branches that have first learned to abide. Our happiness in Jesus's love is his priority for us, even above our sense of being useful to him; in fact, our fruitfulness depends on it.

The Glorious Ones

When Christians enjoy union and communion with the Lord—in private, in families, and in public worship—they are transformed into his likeness (2 Cor. 3:18). Paul writes to the Ephesians that "the manifold wisdom of God" is made known to the heavenly realms "through the church" (3:10). He saw the redeemed and united family of God, Jew and Gentile (2:11–22), as the dwelling place of Christ himself (3:17) and the context for sounding his love, that we might be "filled with all the fullness of God" (3:17–19). Even as we wait for Christ to return one day in glory, we now look for him "and rejoice with joy that is inexpressible and *filled with glory*" (1 Pet. 1:8). This is the reason the glory of God is so often said to dwell *with* and *in* his people. Where the Lord is present with his people, his very own light and life shine out.

> Out of Zion, the perfection of beauty,
> *God shines forth.* (Ps. 50:2)

Contrary to many of our assumptions and experiences, the church *is* glorious with the glory of her Lord. But the glory of the Lord of the church is not slick impressiveness, world domination, or smugness. His—and our—glory is a cruciform glory. It is not a grasping human glory that takes from and hassles the world, but a full, divine glory that gives away the cloak as well as the tunic (Matt. 5:40), passes on the best seats (Matt. 23:6), and welcomes the hungry, thirsty, and naked (Matt. 25:31–40). The church is, by its very nature, *ecstatic*—that is, outgoing and outward-facing, like the Lord. From the beginning, God's choice of a people to be his own was for the sake of the world. Adam and Eve were first placed in Eden to be fruitful and multiply (Gen. 1:18); Abraham was called out and blessed so that he would *be* a blessing to all the families of the earth (Gen. 12:3); the Christian is chosen by Christ and appointed to bear fruit (John 15:16). As Christians, we know ourselves to be chosen not at the *exclusion* of other sinners but to bring them in to share the blessing we ourselves know. For this reason, Peter writes, "But you are a chosen race, a royal priesthood, a holy nation, a people for his own possession, *that* you may proclaim the excellencies of him who called you out of darkness into his marvelous light" (1 Pet. 2:9).

The Lord says:

> You are the light of the world. A city set on a hill cannot be hidden. Nor do people light a lamp and put it under a basket, but on a stand, and it gives light to all in the house. In the same way, *let*

your light shine before others, so that they may see your good works and give glory to your Father who is in heaven. (Matt. 5:14–16)

And to Daniel he said, "Those who are wise shall shine like the brightness of the sky above; and those who turn many to righteousness, like the stars forever and ever" (12:3).

David, after escaping an enemy with his life, wrote that he would constantly bless and praise the Lord: he had sought the Lord, who had answered and delivered him from all his fears (Ps. 34:1–4). "Taste and see that the LORD is good!" he cries (Ps. 34:8); "Come, O children, listen to me," he beckons (Ps. 34:11). His heart is full of the Lord's salvation and blessings so that he cannot keep it all to himself. He proves his own words to be true that "those who look to him are radiant" (Ps. 34:5).

Shining in the Darkness

When the church shines the light of the gospel in the world, we see real action. "The light shines in the darkness," says John, "and the darkness has not overcome it" (John 1:5). Because the light and glory of the church are no secondary light and glory but Christ himself, we can always expect to see the darkness pushed back. This does not necessarily mean instant and obvious success in all our mission: we know that the heralding of Christ is to some the fragrance of death (2 Cor. 2:16) and a two-edged sword (Heb. 4:12) that can harden hearts as well as unlock them (Heb. 3:15). Our mission will sometimes divide, just as Christ divides: "Whoever is not with me is against me, and whoever does not gather with me scatters" (Matt. 12:30). What else could we expect, being bearers of his word and glory?

To take the light of Christ into the world is warfare. The apostles were in no doubt about the essentially military nature of proclamation.

We wrestle "against the rulers, against the authorities, against the cosmic powers over this present darkness, against the spiritual forces of evil in the heavenly places" (Eph. 6:12); we serve as co-laborers and fellow "soldiers" (Phil. 2:25; 2 Tim. 2:1–4); and together we brandish weapons of divine power to bring every thought into obedience to Christ (2 Cor. 10:3–6). Strong in the Lord's mighty power (Eph. 6:10), the church can march out to battle confident that he *will* consume wickedness, sin, and evil. Darkness cannot stand before the advance of the light.

The nature of the church's warfare is not brutish or brash, though. Paul's strong words about "destroying strongholds" and "destroying arguments" set up against Christ are written as he entreats the Corinthians "by the meekness and gentleness of Christ" (2 Cor. 10:1). The strength we show and victory we expect are not any other power and triumph than that of Christ on the cross. We are not like medieval Crusaders who used violence and coercion to batter masses into submission, but with the message of the cross and the demonstration of the Spirit's power (1 Cor. 2:1–5), we serve our captain, *Christ*, in a *Christlike* way.

When I Am Weak

Mission fueled by the fullness of God is able to deal with the weakness of its missionaries. Wounded soldiers, struggling saints, and stumbling preachers are not dismissed from the Lord's army, because they are not expected to be full in and of themselves. In our suffering, our battle with sin, and our lack of experience or boldness or eloquence, we are nonetheless invited to delight ourselves in the Lord and find fullness in him. Paul's experience with weakness led him to know Christ's power in him so deeply that he was content not to feign personal strength but to renounce it.

But he said to me, "My grace is sufficient for you, for my power is made perfect in weakness." Therefore I will boast all the more gladly of my weaknesses, so that the power of Christ may rest upon me. For the sake of Christ, then, I am content with weaknesses, insults, hardships, persecutions, and calamities. For when I am weak, then I am strong. (2 Cor. 12:9–10)

A "missiology of glory" would lean on the evangelists' skills and intellect, emphasize their record or fruitfulness, and promise them satisfaction and reward as a result of their performance. But Paul's is a "missiology of the cross," "carrying in the body the death of Jesus, so that the life of Jesus may also be manifested" in him (2 Cor. 4:10). Here, my individual strengths and weaknesses are equally in the hands of the Lord, who can work through both. To concentrate on my "performance" is a category error, because my delight and satisfaction are in the Lord, who lavishly loves me *before* I set myself to work for him. He does not need my strengths or despise my weaknesses, and this will make me bold in a way I would not naturally be. *His* power is at work in me; *his* life is being manifested through me.

This addresses, too, our ongoing sin. Even good evangelists are not as full as they might be. A "missiology of glory" will look to cover over sins with activism, effectively paying God off with souls saved balanced against our own debt of bad behavior. A "missiology of the cross" accepts the verdict of the cross on all our apparently good works and can look with realism at our polluted motivations, our smug pleasure in being "useful to God," and the instinct to impress others with our culturally sensitive evangelism. Even in our sin—our frequent denial of the Lord and of our new life in him—we are not finally empty but know the fullness of God. His mercies never come to an end, and his compassion does not fail (Lam. 3:22). The same

Son of God who gave himself for us on the cross is, even now, a sympathetic high priest who continues to intercede for us as we struggle with temptation (Heb. 2:14; 4:15; 7:25). His Spirit continues to walk with us (Rom. 8:4), and the Father will always accept us, since we are clothed with indestructible righteousness in Christ (2 Cor. 5:21; Col. 1:21–22). His work for us has *already* justified us, has given us new birth, and now transforms and motivates us. All that is truly good and fruitful in the Christian life flows from our contented fullness in Christ and the glory of his goodness.

Blood and Glory

This matchless love and grace to such empty ones is a fullness that takes us beyond ourselves. Adopted by a perfect Father, united to his glorious Son, and indwelt by the Comforter, Christians are able to take to the spiritual battlefield of mission with happy, humble selflessness. Knowing that his light drives out the darkness before us and his strength overcomes the weakness within us, we can exhibit a bravery that goes beyond our natural personalities or abilities.

Troops that are underfed and flagging will not win a battle, and a town under siege with its supplies cut off will soon fall. But a well-loved, satisfied army will follow their captain into the line of fire, trusting him and eagerly listening to his command. In mission and in ministry, the church of Jesus is never reduced to rations, for our captain is never short on supplies and encourages us constantly to come back to his table for more. Richard Sibbes explains:

> We see, then, that we cannot please Christ better than in shewing ourselves welcome, by cheerful taking part of his rich provision. It is an honour to his bounty to fall to; and it is the temper of spirit that a Christian aims at, to "rejoice always in the Lord." . . . Our

duty is to accept of Christ's inviting of us. What will we do for him, if we will not feast with him? We will not suffer with him, if we will not feast with him; we will not suffer with him, if we will not joy with him, and in him. . . . That which we should labour to bring with us is a taste of these dainties, and an appetite to them. . . . The chief thing that Christ requireth is a good stomach to these dainties.[4]

Christians who delight themselves in Jesus and find themselves amazed at the fullness he has poured into them are willing to give of themselves—to sacrifice, to go with him to the very end. Suffering in Jesus's service is something we are frequently told to expect. Paul writes, "It has been granted to you that for the sake of Christ you should not only believe in him but also suffer for his sake" (Phil. 1:29), and this is, in fact, a participation in Christ's own sufferings, which are a gateway to resurrection life (Phil. 3:10–11). Peter says that "if you are insulted for the name of Christ, you are *blessed, because the Spirit of glory and of God rests upon you*" (1 Pet. 4:14). "Be faithful unto death," says the Lord, "and I will give you the crown of life" (Rev. 2:10). Only when we have seen the glory of the cross can we face taking up our own crosses (Matt. 16:24).

With our eyes on ourselves or our spiritual enemy, we will be easily spooked on the battlefield. We will be afraid and tempted to desert. But marching under the banner of the cross of Jesus, we can never lose heart (2 Cor. 4:1, 16). For on the cross, our captain has gone before us into the fight and has already conquered Satan, sin, and death. He has shed his blood and shown his glory. He has shown us a love

---

4   Richard Sibbes, *The Complete Works of Richard Sibbes*, ed. Alexander B. Grosart, vol. 2 (Edinburgh: Nichol, 1862), 34–35.

that cannot be quenched, even by death (Song 8:6). We cannot lose! At the cross, our cowardice dries up and we are filled with boldness.

This has been the experience of generations of martyrs who have faced wild animals in the arena or watched as the flames licked up their legs at the stake. Even the most fearful and threatened have known something of the joy that was set before Christ that led him to endure the cross and despise its shame (Heb. 12:2). Moses, a naturally timid and hesitant man (Ex. 4:10), "considered the reproach of Christ greater wealth than the treasures of Egypt" (Heb. 11:26) and saw the Egyptian army routed before him. Stephen, standing defenseless and alone before an enraged crowd, was thrown out of the city and stoned to death but saw into heaven as Jesus stood to greet him (Acts 7:54–60). Paul, a naturally unimpressive and underwhelming man (2 Cor. 10:10), was able to take an uncompromising stand against false teachers and their distorted gospels under Christ crucified (1 Cor. 2:2). He considered himself already crucified with Christ and living in him, even as he denied himself (Gal. 2:20).

In the second century, Polycarp, a bishop of Smyrna, in modern day Turkey, was pressed to deny Christ under threat of burning. He famously replied: "Eighty-six years I have been his servant, and he has done me no wrong. How can I blaspheme my King who saved me?"[5] Then he surrendered his body to the flames. All these found Christ to be a King worth living and dying for: not under duress, but delightedly and with boldness. Reginald Heber's verse paints the scene well:

A glorious band, the chosen few
on whom the Spirit came,

---

5 *Martyrdom of Polycarp* 9.3, in *The Apostolic Fathers in English*, trans. and ed. Michael W. Holmes, 3rd ed. (Grand Rapids, MI: Baker Academic, 2006), 150.

twelve valiant saints, their hope they knew,
and mocked the cross and flame:
they met the tyrant's brandished steel,
the lion's gory mane;
they bowed their necks the death to feel:
who follows in their train?[6]

Christians filled with the Spirit and happiness in God are sent out in mission in the train of God's Son. Our journey under his banner is so often through pain, betrayal, depression, persecution, disappointment, blood, sweat, and tears—but it is, nevertheless, a path he has walked before us and now walks with us. It is a path he has sanctified and glorified, and the path to the eternal rest of heaven.

Outside the Camp

A missionary emptied of herself and full of Christ becomes a radiantly outgoing person. Like the Lord, she is able to go out from herself in blessing the world where there is no blessing. Christ's fullness so fills her that she can flow out, sharing the knowledge of the one who has so blessed her. In this way, mission is truly glorious and outshining. The world opens up before believers as we long to see the glory of our God resounding and redounding in the world.

In the law, the camp of Israel and her cities were to be kept ceremonially clean, and all that was defiled had to be ejected. Outside the camp was the only fit place for throwing out ashes and waste (Lev. 4:21); it was the colony of those afflicted with infectious diseases (Lev. 13:46) and the venue for the execution of blasphemers (Lev. 24:14). Situated at a distance from the tabernacle and the homes of God's

---

6 Reginald Heber, "The Son of God Goes Forth to War" (1812), https://hymnary.org.

people, it stood for uncleanness, exclusion, and death. No Israelite could touch a dead thing (Lev. 11:31) or soiled bed sheets (Lev. 15:7) or someone unclean with a disease (Lev. 5:3). Uncleanness spreads and infects, like the yeast of the Pharisees (Matt. 16:6), and the law was designed to strictly demarcate not only clean and unclean but also *life and death*. To touch a corpse or mold and decay was to touch death, and the people of Israel belonged to the *living* God. So many of Moses's commands taught this point.

Yet Jesus went out from the center to the unclean: to prostitutes and tax collectors, lepers and Gentiles. Without being infected or compromised, he embraced them, welcomed them, and saved them. In fact, he himself "suffered outside the [city] gate" on the cross to make his people holy (Heb. 13:12). Because he is so full of purity and holiness, he was not diminished by touching death and disease, but his life blazed out, cleansing and healing, delivering, and making whole. He drove out not just unclean spirits but death itself.

Our own mission now is to "*go to him outside the camp* and bear the reproach he endured" (Heb. 13:13). Made alive, filled, and sanctified in Christ, we do not hide within the "camp" of the church but reach out. Now, with the sword of the Spirit, we too drive out death, even in the very places it seems most at home. This outward stretching of the church, matching that of her Lord, is the extension of his kingdom and blessing into the world, his light shining, and his goodness spreading. Cozy huddles of inward-looking Christians, maintaining church programs and diligently avoiding any contact with the outside world, are pushing *against* the church's fundamental calling. The "holier than thou" can sometimes appear to rival Jesus's own holiness, but they actually undermine it. His holiness is not vulnerable and in need of protection by his people, as though it might be overwhelmed by the sin of the world. It does not retreat in the face of uncleanness but is death-defying in its explosive outward motion. Christ's church always moves into the world with a holiness that can bless, purify, and give life.

A Band of Brothers

Finally, this outward, selfless posture of the church in mission extends to those we find alongside us in the ranks. In a people filled with Jesus's all-embracing glory, there can be no room for tribalism, competition, and hidden agendas. The Lord prayed for our unity right up to the night of his death (John 17:21). Personality clashes, empire building, the bearing of grudges, and dark whispering about one another do not belong.

Unhappy, empty mission is marked by selfishness. It is only if I am fixated on myself that another is a threat or a competitor. It is only if I am frantically covering up my emptiness that I lie to my friends about how I really am when they ask me. Stinting, self-absorbed pastors and missionaries preach by their lives a stinting, self-absorbed God, rather than the God who generously shines out. If I am delightedly filled by Christ, then I will happily march out shoulder to shoulder with brothers and sisters. If I believe that I am brilliant but you are weak, I will trek out alone without any care for you. But if I know my own wretched sinfulness and emptiness, I will be honored to go *together* with you. I will see Christ in you and feel amazed that I can count you a fellow laborer in the gospel (Phil. 2:25). Then, with honesty, humility, trust, and mutual encouragement, we will go out in mission as a happy fellowship.

Deep Down Delighting

Healthy, robust mission is never an accessory to knowing God. It is not an activist project that must be *added* to our enjoyment of him in salvation. Mission that is to be full and not empty flows only from the satisfaction we experience in Jesus Christ. He will bear our weaknesses, cover our sins, and glorify our suffering for his own sake. This is the promise he has made to his church. Picturing the bride as the marching army of the exodus, Solomon writes,

> Who is this who looks down like the dawn,
>> beautiful as the moon, bright as the sun,
>> awesome as an army with banners? (Song 6:10)

She is the same one he sees

> coming up from the wilderness,
>> leaning on her beloved. (Song 8:5)

For healthy mission, the church must lean hard on her captain, even as she marches. The Reformers spoke of the church constantly reforming—never settling, never getting lazy, either in her knowledge of God or in her mission. Our fullness will always be a matter of filling our eyes with the light of the glory of God in Christ. It is *Christ* that distinguishes the church from the Rotarians or Scouts, making us more than a club with a laudable objective. It is *Christ* who shows us God as he truly is: full, rich, and delightful. Those who satisfy themselves in Christ will be the best missionaries; and the best missionaries will be those most deeply delighted in his love for them.

The fullness of God given to us in salvation sends us out in mission, but even as we go, we are drawn *toward* fullness too. Our present delight in God magnetically leads us toward the day when we will know his love not in part but in whole. The victories we see in mission as his kingdom advances anticipate the day the whole earth will see his glory.

8

We Will See Him as He Is

THE CULMINATION OF MISSION IS GLORY.

Scripture's descriptions of our future hope are crammed with the language of glory.

The Lord calls us to "his own *kingdom and glory*" (1 Thess. 2:12). Paul weighs our present suffering against "the *glory* that is to be revealed to us" (Rom. 8:18). The promised land of Canaan once pictured our future home by being "the most *glorious* of all lands" (Ezek. 20:6; Heb. 4:8). Habakkuk prophesied that

> the earth will be filled
>> with the knowledge of the glory of the LORD
>> as the waters cover the sea. (2:14)

But what will this glory be like? Often when we try to imagine our life in eternity, we soon begin to ponder nervous, slightly guilty questions: Will I recognize my friends and family? Will my dog be there? Will I actually *enjoy* it? Glory filling the earth is all very well, but if all we are looking forward to is a world of sparkling streets and angel harps gleaming in the sunshine, we could be forgiven for thinking it does not sound very attractive.

Underneath our fears is the suspicion that when God finally and fully reveals his glory—the weight and substance of his being and nature—it will turn out to be something *other* than the grace, goodness, and kindness displayed in the gospel. The self-giving glory of the cross will have been simply a means to another end: perhaps God's retirement to a life of isolated majesty, with troublesome humanity out of his hair. He will have finished being good to us, and so we will spend eternity grateful to be saved from judgment, but twiddling our thumbs.

Wonderfully, we could not be more wrong about God's plans.

The Revelation of Jesus Christ

The last book of the Bible is specifically about "the revelation of Jesus Christ" (Rev. 1:1) because it is *his* glory that will be fully unveiled on the last day. All the promises of God—including those about our future—find their "Yes" *in Jesus* (2 Cor. 1:20), meaning that God's plan for "the coming ages" is not to surprise us with a glory other than his Son's but to take us ever deeper into "the immeasurable riches of his grace in kindness toward us in Christ Jesus" (Eph. 2:7). In other words, in the gospel's promised future, we will eternally enjoy the very glory that fuels our lives and mission today.

Our *present* enjoyment of this glory is only partial, since we only see in part (1 Cor. 13:12). There will be joy and wonder we cannot imagine when, on that day, the skies are ripped open and we see him *as he is*, knowing *fully* even as we are fully known (1 Cor. 13:12). But make no mistake, we await "the appearing of the glory of *our great God and Savior*" (Titus 2:13), not the glory of anyone other than Christ crucified.

Jesus showed his friends the scars on his hands and side to prove he was truly alive, filling their hearts with gladness (John 20:20).

The wounds that tell the story of his love mark his resurrected body, which ascended into heaven, and they will define our resurrection life too when he returns.

When he comes, the spark of our *present* enjoyment of God and his gospel will be fanned into flame as all creation is saturated with the glory of our own dear Lord Jesus, the radiance of the Father. All will see the glory of the Savior who laid down his life for sinners, the glory of God who is always full and always blessing.

Since we are sure of our future in the eternal embrace of Jesus Christ, we are people of hope. In our mission today, we invite the sinful, broken, and empty not to the hope of "heaven" as an ethereal afterlife but to the beauty, fullness, and glory of the Lamb who was slain for us. His delight is to fill his people with joy in him both now and *forever*. The glory that we long for and hold out to the world is the very same outshining glory that propels our mission today.

God's Last Great End

This glorious end to the story is both the goal and the motivation of mission because it has *always* been God's design and intention for his creation. From the very beginning to the very end, God's purpose in all things is the demonstration of his glory: this was God's mission before it was ever ours.

Jonathan Edwards says that in Scripture, "God's name and his glory" are spoken of as "his last great end."[1] He takes God's name and glory to mean the same thing: the "manifestation, publication and

---

1 Jonathan Edwards, "The End for Which God Created the World," in *The Works of Jonathan Edwards*, vol. 8, *Ethical Writings*, ed. Paul Ramsey (New Haven, CT: Yale University Press, 1989), 475. "End," here, means "goal" or "purpose."

knowledge" of God's excellency and honor.[2] For example, in Isaiah 48:11, the Lord speaks of the salvation of Israel this way:

> For my own sake, for my own sake, I do it,
>> for how should my name be profaned?
> My glory I will not give to another.

Above all, God seeks, values, and delights in his own glory. The great crescendos of Scripture often come to rest on this theme. The litany of blessings poured on believers in Ephesians 1 are "to the praise of his glory" (v. 14), while Romans 11 shows God himself as both the original source and the *culmination* of everything: "For from him and through him and to him are all things. To him be glory forever. Amen" (v. 36). The glory of God is the bottom line of history.

Edwards is very clear about what this does and does not mean. The God who has been so selflessly kind to us throughout history is not planning to exit stage left with a selfish flourish of megalomania. The final manifestation of his glory is not a last-minute change of direction. No, says Edwards, God's "end" of the display of his own glory involves the *happiness of his people*.[3] God has determined that his own outshining *brings about* our delight and joy in the end. How can this be? Can these two goals really be united without pulling in different directions?

A contrast may help us here. France's King Louis XIV (1638–1715) was famous for seeking his own glory. Living in outrageous opulence, he claimed to be semidivine, calling himself the "Sun King" after the Greek god Apollo, and split his time between starting wars and taking mistresses. On being king, he once wrote:

2 Edwards, *Works*, 8:524.
3 Edwards, *Works*, 8:476.

When one has the State in view, one is working for oneself. . . . When the State is happy, eminent and powerful, he who is cause thereof is covered with glory, and . . . has a right to enjoy all that is most agreeable in life in a greater degree than his subjects, in proportion to his position and theirs.[4]

Being the king ruling over his people was essentially an opportunity for self-indulgence. Even when he wanted good things for France, it was so that he could have the best for himself. Seeking the good of his country was really a way to satiate his appetites and surround himself with pleasure. Louis wanted his people to be happy, but only so that he could be *more* happy than they, building his own happiness on theirs. While his splendor was very obvious to his subjects as he built the magnificent Palace of Versailles and paraded through each day in astonishingly intricate ritual (people would pay to watch the king washed and shaved in the morning), he clearly saw himself quite set apart from the masses in his lofty position. In a sense, he was *using* his people: he had no true concern for their welfare and did not love them—but he did *need* them.

How different it is when the Lord seeks his own glory! When God makes himself and his own glory the finale of history, it is not due to any selfish or callous urge in him. God is not out to *gather* from us some glory he does not have, nor simply to call our attention to his excellence. Unlike Louis XIV, God is not empty and so dependent on us and plotting to take from us. Rather, his plan is to manifest and *share* his glorious fullness with his people. We are to be *partakers* in the glory that is to be revealed (1 Pet. 5:1).

---

4 From *On the Craft of Kingship*, 1679, quoted in Tim Blanning, *The Pursuit of Glory: Europe 1648–1815* (London: Penguin, 2008), 562–63.

Edwards writes of God's "internal" glory "emanating" from him; that is, the weight and richness of all he is in himself in eternity being "communicated" or "exhibited" to us.[5] This is how the display of his own glory is actually one and the same goal for God as the happiness of his people. God is *already* eternally happy in fellowship with his Son, and *that* is what will overflow to us. God will make us eternally happy out of the sheer abundance of his own happiness. It is not a way of keeping us quiet or getting something out of us; quite the opposite, it is something God freely *wants* to do and will do without interruption and infinitely. "God's disposition to communicate good, or to cause his own infinite fullness to flow forth," says Edwards, is really nothing other than God's *goodness* to us, a communication of the very glory in which he himself finds delight.[6] God's own life—the glory he has delighted in for eternity—will be our own.

Gracious Glory

To speak of God giving us his life must send our minds rushing back to the cross, where the Father gave up his Son for us all (Rom. 8:32), and where the Son "loved us and gave himself up for us" (Eph. 5:2). The life we are to receive on resurrection morning is exactly what Christ has purchased for us by his death. On the final day, we will receive full and final delivery of that happiness and healing for which we now have only a deposit. The inheritance, at long last, will be released to amazed beneficiaries. All that Jesus has won for us will come into our possession (Eph. 1:14).

Yet the cross is not simply the *mechanism* by which we receive a selection box of blessings of the new creation: the cross shows us exactly

5 Edwards, *Works*, 8:515.
6 Edwards, *Works*, 8:460.

what *sort* of blessing this is. For the glory of God that will fill the earth at the end is the same glory we see in the death of Jesus. Specifically, the *self-giving* glory of the cross is the key to understanding the glory that is to come. Edwards writes that the happiness God has in mind for us in the age to come is "happiness in union with himself."[7] In other words, Christians will not be sitting on the sidelines as God enjoys being God at a distance. He will not be manifesting his glory to rub our faces in it. Unlike Louis, the King of kings wants to be known and enjoyed by his subjects, giving us *himself* without reservation or limit.

That God should meet our sin and hard-heartedness with forgiveness is one thing; that he should flood the world with his own blessed life and joy is another. That he should do so by pouring out his own blood is beyond our comprehension (Acts 20:28). The glorious mission of the living God is to draw us into the loving fellowship of his own eternal life. Here is Richard Sibbes:

> Do we entertain Christ to our loss? Doth he come empty? No; he comes with all grace. His goodness is a communicative, diffusive goodness. He comes to spread his treasures, to enrich the heart with all grace and strength, to bear all afflictions, to encounter all dangers, to bring peace of conscience, and joy in the Holy Ghost. He comes, indeed, to make our hearts, as it were, a heaven. Do but consider this. He comes not for his own ends; but to empty his goodness into our hearts. As a breast that desires to empty itself when it is full; so this fountain hath the fulness of a fountain, which strives to empty his goodness into our souls. He comes out of love to us.[8]

---

7 Edwards, *Works*, 8:533.
8 Richard Sibbes, *The Complete Works of Richard Sibbes*, ed. Alexander B. Grosart, vol. 2 (Edinburgh: Nichol, 1862), 67.

Jesus's description of our "eternal life" in John 17:3 is specifically about enjoying this fellowship with God: "that they know you, the only true God, and Jesus Christ whom you have sent." He earlier promised his disciples that if anyone would love him and keeps his word, then "my Father will love him, and we will come to him and *make our home with him*" (John 14:23). The life and glory that will one day fill the earth springs from the fountain of the everlasting love and delight of the Father, Son, and Spirit. The outgoing, other-centered joy that God has eternally known will be mapped out onto history and onto the lives of redeemed sinners.

In this glory, we who are naturally far from God and tragically self-absorbed will be made eternally joyful and content, enfolded into indestructible fellowship with God. We who are in Christ will be drawn in to know and enjoy him further and more deeply than ever before, knowing in full what we now know only in part, seeing with crisp clarity what we now see only dimly of his beauty (1 Cor. 13:12). We and all creation will come to enjoy true life in unending communion with God. For God himself will come to *dwell with us* (Rev. 21:3), and we will marvel at him (2 Thess. 1:10) and be with him forever (1 Thess. 4:17). The one who once came as a "friend of tax collectors and sinners" (Luke 7:34) and loved them to death will prove himself devoted to us for endless ages.

Allah's paradise in Islam promises rivers of wine and no more work to do as attractive benefits,[9] but is much thinner on the prospect of actually *seeing* and enjoying Allah. His presence is seemingly not the draw. In the new creation, though, John writes that God's servants will "need no light of lamp or sun, for *the Lord God will be their*

---

9 Qur'an 47:15; 35:35.

light" (Rev. 22:5). The treasure and glory of heaven is God himself. On the last day, God will not be doling out bargain-basement blessings with a long-handled spoon: all that is good in the age to come is the direct result of his giving *himself* to us. Our preoccupation in glory will not be God's blessings in themselves, but the blessed God. Anne Cousin's hymn, inspired by the letters of Samuel Rutherford, captures this beautifully:

> The bride eyes not her garment,
> but her dear bridegroom's face;
> I will not gaze at glory,
> but on my King of grace;
> not at the crown he gifteth,
> but on his piercèd hand:
> the Lamb is all the glory
> of Emmanuel's land.[10]

On the last day, just as at Calvary, God who is full of life, light, and love will *pour himself out* for those who are empty, gloomy, and unlovely. Flowing to us from the cross, his is an entirely *gracious* glory.

Heaven, God's home, is filled with his glory now. Stephen gazed into it and saw the glory of God there (Acts 7:55). Asaph speaks of being received into God's glory at his death (Ps. 73:24). When Christians die, we often say they have "gone to glory." Yet, in John's vision of the last day in Revelation 21:10–11, he saw this glory descending to earth. He describes "the holy city Jerusalem coming down out of heaven from God, *having the glory of God.*" When Christ returns, our beloved departed saints will return with him (Jude 14), quite

---

10   Anne Ross Cousin, "The Sands of Time Are Sinking" (1857), https://hymnary.org.

literally bringing heaven to earth. Then the glory of heaven, God's dwelling place, will bathe the world in God's own light and beauty.

The hope we treasure, and invite others to in our mission, is the climax of the gospel of Jesus manifested on the earth. The Lord's own brilliant fullness will surge out into *all* that is now empty, pitiful, and poor. When he comes, all that is presently distorted and broken by sin will be untwisted and made whole. Sadness and shame will be banished. Glorious day will chase away the night as the Lord shines, bringing his salvation to bear on all things. Our bodies will be transformed and glorified (1 Cor. 15:42–52), bidding goodbye to illness, weakness, and disability. The creation, too, will be freed from its sin-induced bondage to corruption (Rom. 8:21) so that rocks that have never cried out in praise (Luke 19:40) will then burst into song (Isa. 44:23), and the trees will applaud with joy (Isa. 55:12). The radiant presence of God himself will drive out darkness, death, and sin; there simply will not be room for them as the whole world reels and resounds with his glory. Isaac Watts said of Jesus,

> He comes to make his blessings flow
> far as the curse is found.[11]

Not a single grain of sand or one blade of grass in all the world—and no hair on your head—will escape the tide of renewing blessing that will sweep over the earth.

No lingering shadow of darkness will be unlit, no residue of curse and evil will cling on, and none of the goodness dammed up in the heart of our Father will be kept back from us. The full effects of his Son's glorious Easter victory that, for now, he only contains in heaven

---

11 Isaac Watts, "Joy to the World" (1719), https://hymnary.org.

out of merciful patience with the lost (2 Pet. 3:9) he will finally and gladly unleash upon us.

All Things New

The personal presence of the Lord, finally manifested to the creation in all his fullness, will mean that all that has saddened and hurt us will be blasted away. The Lamb on heaven's throne will declare, "Behold, I am making all things new" (Rev. 21:5), so transforming will his presence be to his broken creation. He promises that God himself "will wipe away every tear from their eyes, and death shall be no more, neither shall there be mourning, nor crying, nor pain anymore, for the former things have passed away" (Rev. 21:4). He will finally drive out Satan and all evil from the world, and they will never be able to torment and harm God's people again (Rev. 20:10). Death, the final enemy, will be destroyed, and all will be perfect, everlasting life (1 Cor. 15:26).

What a hope to share with the world! In the drying of our tears, we see a God so filled with compassion that he personally stoops to comfort his people. In the last defeat of Satan, we see a God so beautifully pure that he will tolerate nothing that would harm his children. In the end of death, we see a God so generously full that he loves to give his life without measure such that death is blotted out forever. The hope of his coming is comfort for the weeping, the oppressed, and the dying today. *As we hold out the hope of the gospel in our broken world now, it is the full revelation of the loving God of the gospel that we anticipate.*

Seeing all this, Isaiah set the scene of an exultant celebration of the end of death, tears, and shame. He foresaw an international banquet, stocked with the choicest foods and the best wine, with its venue set to be the mountain of the Lord—God's own place. Here, the redeemed will raise a toast:

Behold, this is our God; we have waited for him, that he might
    save us.
This is the LORD; we have waited for him;
    let us be glad and rejoice in his salvation. (25:9)

For now, in our fallen world, even as we enjoy a dinner party, we're aware that we have to be back at our desks on Monday morning. We cannot enjoy holidays without also suffering tiredness, travel sickness, and chairs at the table once occupied by loved ones now hauntingly empty. We cannot revel in our successes without the parallel track of our failure and weaknesses. The good things we enjoy presently come to an end. Cherished relationships break down. All of our lives are lived in this shadow, such that even the happiest, most carefree days can be snuffed out by a crashing disappointment or a phone call with spine-chilling news.

But a day is coming when the shadow will be lifted. You will have cried your last tear, grappled with guilt's last assault, suffered your last bereavement. For when the glory of the Lord fills the earth, we will live in a world with no more threat of danger, disease, and death. Satan, suffering, and sin will be distant memories to us as we come to enjoy God, one another, and the creation just as we were meant to. We will know full and everlasting joy, sharing the glory of the eternal, blessed happiness of Father, Son, and Spirit (1 Tim. 1:11). We ourselves will be made *like God* as we enjoy final and complete union with him (1 John 3:2).

A World of Love

The defining characteristic of our future fellowship with God is his love for us. For God *is* love (1 John 4:8) and "love never ends" (1 Cor. 13:8). Knowing the love of God is the heartbeat of our fellowship with him now and will be the theme of our songs for all eternity. Preaching on 1 Corinthians 13:8, Edwards noted that while the other gifts and fruits of the Spirit (prophecy, tongues, knowledge) will pass away eventually, love will remain forever. Love is greater even than faith and hope (1 Cor. 13:13), because when our faith is turned to sight and our hope is fulfilled, we will never be finished with the love of God.

Edwards writes that heaven, God's home, is a "world of love" because the God of love lives there. "The glorious presence of God in heaven fills heaven with love, as the sun placed in the midst of the hemisphere in a clear day fills the world with light."[12] Just as every person's home bears the marks of his or her ownership and influence, so heaven will "remarkably show forth the beauty and loveliness of God and Christ" and have the sparkle of divine love.[13] As surely as we pray for God's kingdom to come and his will to be done "on earth as it is in heaven" (Matt. 6:10), love will be the defining characteristic of the new creation. The infinite love and light of God will dispel all hate and ugliness as the Spirit will still be "poured forth in perfect love into every heart."[14]

This means that our love for God will suddenly skyrocket. We will love God more truly because we will finally have an unclouded appreciation of his love for us. Knowing how he has loved us from all eternity, and having received the prize of our faith, we will love him sinlessly and with a depth of gratitude we have not yet experienced. Especially, we will love God more because we will understand the cross more profoundly. The saints

---

12 Edwards, *Works*, 8:369.
13 Edwards, *Works*, 8:382.
14 Edwards, *Works*, 8:367.

shall know that he has loved them with a dying [sacrificial] love. They shall then be more sensible than they are now what great love it manifested in Christ, that he should lay down his life for them. Then Christ will open to their view the great fountain of love in his heart far beyond what they ever before saw.[15]

Under the influence of this new realization, our love for others will also be transformed. The very light by which we *see and understand* all things will be "the light of love," because it is "the shining of the glory of the Lamb of God, that most wonderful influence of lamblike meekness and love which fills the heavenly Jerusalem with light."[16] In this light, nothing and nobody will be unlovely, since we will all absorb the humility of the Lamb, seeing everyone else beautified in the glory of God. Wherever we turn our eyes, whatever and whoever we see, we will see "nothing but beauty and glory."[17] Here, finally, we will see the church beautified as a bride and presented to her bridegroom and head in unblemished splendor (Eph. 5:27). Says Edwards:

There is to be seen a glorious heavenly Father, a glorious Redeemer; there is to be felt and possessed a glorious Sanctifier. All the persons who belong to that blessed society are lovely. The Father of the family is so, and so are all his children. The Head of the body is so, and so are all the members.[18]

For the first time, we all will be perfectly loved, lovely, and loving, just as our God is. All our relationships will be characterized

---

15 Edwards, *Works*, 8:377.
16 Edwards, *Works*, 8:382.
17 Edwards, *Works*, 8:371.
18 Edwards, *Works*, 8:370.

by this loveliness: no falling out, no jealousy, no secret disdain for one another. "There shall be no string out of tune to cause any jar in the harmony of that world, no unpleasant note to cause any discord."[19] The love we now receive and return to others is stained by the self-centered motivations that can so easily pollute even our most sincere affection. But in satisfied happiness in God's presence, we will be humble and holy saints, honestly rejoicing to see others glorified and happy, even those who may receive greater reward than we do (Mark 10:40). We will never doubt the love of others for us as we are so prone to do here, because their love and ours will be pure and perfect, without the sneaking suspicion of flattery or faking.[20] All the insecurities and fears that now plague our friendships and relationships will be dispelled as we stand with humble dignity in the presence of God and of our brothers and sisters.

The future we have to offer to our friends and neighbors is a world of unshakeable, unquenchable love. Can you imagine a life where you *know*, without any creeping anxiety, that you are perfectly and totally loved by God? Where you love him in return without any whisper of shame or inadequacy? A life where you are entirely secure in the love of those around you and are able to love them all without feeling exposed or vulnerable? Where you love people with such a generous freedom that you yourself only become more open and lovely? This is life in the glory of God and the light of the Lamb who was slain.

This is all pure, incomprehensible mercy to us. Here is paradise itself bestowed on the undeserving and ungrateful. Here is an ocean of blessing direct from the heart of God, deluged on sinners who had

19 Edwards, *Works*, 8:371.
20 Edwards, *Works*, 8:378.

hated him. Once alienated from him and far from all his blessings, we have been brought near and adopted in Christ, and filled with the Spirit as a guarantee of *this* future. The grace we have found at the foot of the cross we will discover again and again in wave after infinite wave: the free giving of the superabundant one to those who are empty, needy, and longing.

Children of the Light

The promise of this life before us sustains us now in our ministry and mission. And it is precisely this hope that we hold out to the world. Today, Edwards says, we live in "a world of storms and tempests, a world of pride, and selfishness, and envy, and malice, and scorn, and contempt, and contention and war," where there is little relief for us. Ahead of us, like the Israelites standing at the Jordan looking into the promised land, is a "Canaan of rest" we know we will one day enter.[21] This hope before us defines us now, for in bringing us to new life in Christ, the Spirit has brought down "some of that light, and some of that holy pure flame, which is in the world of love, . . . giving it place" in us.[22] The Christian life is, by definition, a foretaste and foreshadowing of the glory of heaven, as our hearts are drawn to God and flow out to others in "humble spiritual love."[23] Our desires, tastes, behavior, and hope are increasingly shaped by the Spirit to preempt the glorious future that is ours in Jesus.

Our mission carries the same glory as our hope. In 1 Thessalonians 5, Paul calls Christians "children of light," who do not belong to the darkness of this present and passing age (vv. 4–6). We live in the

---

21 Edwards, *Works*, 8:385.
22 Edwards, *Works*, 8:387–88.
23 Edwards, *Works*, 8:388.

world as "strangers and exiles," having a life that runs entirely counter to its ways, seeking our heavenly homeland (Heb. 11:13–14). Many around us sense and suffer the wickedness of the world, but they cannot understand why it is as painful and disturbing as it is—nor that they themselves are part of the reason for the state of things. The god of this age has blinded unbelievers, Paul says, to the gospel of Jesus's glory (2 Cor. 4:4), and spiritual powers now hold the world in captivity to "empty deceit" (Col. 2:8). Because believers are filled with the life of Christ by the Spirit, we are lights in "this present darkness" (Eph. 6:12), beacons of divine glory in a sea of emptiness. We are those whose birth, way of life, and inheritance are marked by the glory of God. In a sense, Christians are children of the future, living in the world with their sights set beyond it, knowing what is coming soon. Our very presence in the spiritual darkness of this age is a warning to it of its own downfall (Phil. 1:28).

In this way, the whole of the Christian life is ordered by God's glory. It begins when Jesus, the radiance of the Father's glory, meets us in his self-giving on the cross, and it will find its fulfillment when that same self-giving glory covers the earth. In the meantime, our lives now are foretastes of what is to come. As we gaze on Christ's glory and are filled with his Spirit, we are conformed to his image, and we are demonstrating to the watching world the nature of the life to come. Our way of life in the church and our witness to the world are glorified and beautified as we grow into the likeness of his humility, kindness, and love. We are proleptic, prophetic witnesses of the glory that is to come. As we lift up his cross, making ourselves happy in him, we will see men, women, and children drawn to his light—every new disciple a new point of light in the darkness. As we express unity, love, and compassion to one another, we taste something of the perfect love of the age to come.

The church's mission is shaped and driven by the very nature of our God. All that we know of him, however limited by our present ignorance and sin, fills us with joy. Yet our hope of knowing him fully in the age to come can only increase our delight and anticipation, propelling us out into the world in overwhelmed gladness. How can we leave our friends, families, and colleagues in ignorance of the Lord whose purpose for all things is so good? Knowing his love that has reached out to us—and will one day reach out and fill all the world—what else can we do but reach out with that same love today? Gazing on the glory of the Lamb who was slain for us, and knowing that *this* is the glory that will shine in all the world, we may well sing with Wesley,

> 'Tis all my business here below
> to cry, "Behold the Lamb!"[24]

Happily Ever After

There is a reason that all the best stories end with a bride and groom living happily ever after: it is the one true story in the universe. At the end, Jesus Christ will fulfill his vows to his church, "All that I am, I give to you, and all that I have I share with you." The glorious fullness of God will be ours forever, and we will find unending delight in our husband. This was his great purpose from the beginning of all things. Edwards writes,

> The creation of the world seems to have been especially for this end, that the eternal Son of God might obtain a spouse, towards whom he might fully exercise the infinite benevolence of his nature, and to whom he might, as it were, open and pour forth all that

---

24 Charles Wesley, "Jesus! the Name High over All" (1749), https://hymnary.org.

immense fountain of condescension, love and grace that was in his heart, and that in this way God might be glorified.[25]

The final mention of the Lamb in the book of Revelation comes in chapter 21 when John is invited by an angel, "Come, I will show you the Bride, the wife of the Lamb" (v. 9). He is carried away by the Spirit to "a great, high mountain," where he sees "the holy city Jerusalem coming down out of heaven from God, *having the glory of God*, its radiance like a most rare jewel" (vv. 10–11). The Lamb on the throne has been married to the bride he purchased with his blood. Their new and heavenly marital city-home is indelibly inscribed with the names of his people (v. 14), the reward of his suffering. His work is finished, the union is complete, and his glorified bride is his forever. This had been his heart's desire from the beginning (Song 2:10; Hos. 2:20). This was surely "the joy that was set before him," which enabled him to endure the cross (Heb. 12:2).

Yes, the culmination of history is the glory of God. Not glory taken but glory *given*. The whole creation suffused with his light, his creatures filled and made happy in his goodness, his bride drenched eternally in his love. We, the redeemed, can only sing,

Worthy is the Lamb who was slain,
to receive power and wealth and wisdom and might
and honor and glory and blessing! (Rev. 5:12)

To him who sits on the throne and to the Lamb
be blessing and honor and glory and might forever and ever!
(Rev. 5:13)

---

25 Jonathan Edwards, *The Works of Jonathan Edwards*, vol. 25, *Sermons and Discourses, 1743–1758*, ed. Wilson H. Kimnach (New Haven, CT: Yale University Press, 2006), 187.

General Index

Scripture Index

Union

We fuel reformation in churches and lives.

Union Publishing invests in the next generation of leaders with theology that gives them a taste for a deeper knowledge of God. From books to our free online content, we are committed to producing excellent resources that will refresh, transform, and grow believers and their churches.

We want people everywhere to know, love, and enjoy God, glorifying him in everything they do. For this reason, we've collected hundreds of free articles, podcasts, book chapters, and video content for our free online collection. We also produce a fresh stream of written, audio, and video resources to help you to be more fully alive in the truth, goodness, and beauty of Jesus.

If you are hungry for reformational resources that will help you delight in God and grow in Christ, we'd love for you to visit us at unionpublishing.org.

unionpublishing.org

Union Series

Full & Concise Editions

Rejoice and Tremble | *What Does It Mean to Fear the Lord?*

Deeper | *How Does God Change Us?*

The Loveliest Place | *Why Should We Love the Local Church?*

God Shines Forth | *What Fuels the Mission of the Church?*

The Union series invites readers to experience deeper enjoyment of God through four interconnected values: delighting in God, growing in Christ, serving the church, and blessing the world.

For more information, visit **crossway.org**.